ELVIS PRESLEY

Collected

Written by

Michael O'Neill & Carolyn Thomas

BOOKS

First Published Danann Publishing Ltd 2019

WARNING: For private domestic use only, any unauthorised Copying, hiring, lending or public performance of this book is illegal.

CAT NO: DAN0449

Photography courtesy of

Getty images:

ullstein bild	Terry O'Neill
CBS Photo Archive	National Archives / Handout
Michael Ochs Archives / Handout	Fotos International
Bettmann	RB/Redferns
Hulton Archive / Stringer	Steve Morley
GAB Archive	Archive Photos / Stringer
Movie Poster Image Art	Ben Mancuso
Sunset Boulevard	Movie Poster Image Art
Don Cravens	Don Cravens/The LIFE Images Collection

Other images Wiki Commons

Book layout & design Darren Grice at Ctrl-d

Copy Editor Tom O'Neill

Made in EU.

ISBN: 978-1-912332-36-6

CONTENTS

INTRODUCTION

Simply the words, "the King", will conjure up a thousand images, a thousand thoughts in the minds of a generation of young guys and gals who were suddenly liberated from the oppressive moral strictures imposed on them by their parents and teachers in the 1950s. This "beautiful, astonishingly beautiful" young man, electrified girls and boys alike with his on-stage gyrations that left little to the imagination of a horrified older generation fed on the superbly calming talents of Bing Crosby and Frank Sinatra and their ilk, whose mellow tones were reassuring to a generation that had come through almost a half-century of troubled decades.

Yet Elvis didn't discard his predecessors' well-trodden paths completely; he, too, could croon with the best of them, albeit with the velvet undertones of a dangerous seducer. He covered songs, employed musical components and adapted the singing style used by a man he sincerely admired, and who could be considered the Elvis of his time, Dean Martin! In fact, Elvis dubbed Martin "The King of Cool" and adopted Martin's relaxed-mischievous stage persona and obvious enjoyment in displaying his talent.

But Elvis's own trail-blazing artistry and popularity forced those who had gone before him to change tack as far as they were able. Dean Martin, for example, according to writer Nick Tosches, became a serious actor once Elvis had assumed the mantel of young, easy-going singer-in-chief. Perhaps the incomparable influence of Elvis Presley on the music world can best be summed up in the first and subsequent comments by those crooners into whose ordered world he burst like an atomic augmented fifth. Bing Crosby began by affirming that, "Elvis will never contribute a damn thing to music". But once the new wave had swept over him, he was wise enough to realise that, "Elvis helped to kill off the influence of me and my contemporaries, but I respect him for that." Because, Crosby added, "no one could have opened the door to the future like he did".

The inimitable Frank Sinatra's attitude in the 1950s was, "His kind of music is deplorable, a rancid smelling aphrodisiac... It fosters almost totally negative and destructive reactions in young people". Sinatra's tune then mellowed into superlatives; "Elvis was the embodiment of the whole American culture. Life wouldn't have been the same without him".

Those singers who came after him had no need to recant on their initial reactions. From Mick Jagger's "No one, but no one is his equal or ever will be. He was and is supreme", to John Lennon's "Before Elvis there was nothing... if there hadn't been an Elvis there wouldn't have been the Beatles", everyone recognises in Elvis Presley a brave and superbly talented giant of the musical world whose love of success and luxury brought the life of a gentle man and a confused soul to a sad, indeed, tragic conclusion.

This book will retrace the meteoric rise and fall of this fast-living and glowing star.

9

Elvis performs during his second appearance on 'The Ed Sullivan Show,' New York, October 28, 1956

"YOU DON'T KNOW ME."

At around 5 a.m. on the morning of the 8th January 1935, Jesse Garon Presley was stillborn. His brother, Elvis Aron Presley, born just thirty minutes earlier, would manage 42 years of extraordinary life before he followed the brother he had never known over to the other side at 3.30 p.m. on August 16th 1977.

Elvis always wondered about his brother and the relationship they might have had. Did Elvis, a man so completely alone and lonely in his superstardom, also wonder if Jesse might have been a much-needed anchor for his brother in those times of agonising self-doubt and fear?

Elvis's mother tried to assuage both her own distress at the loss of her second child and cover Elvis's bewildered question about why he had lived and Jessie had died, by instilling in her firstborn the belief that he was special. And from the time that he was old enough to understand, Elvis did believe this to be so. In later years he would say, *"From the time I was a kid, I always knew something was going to happen to me. Didn't know exactly what"*.

Elvis came into the world in the poorest state of the American union; in the town of Tupelo, Mississippi. There was no running water or electricity in the Presley's frame house that stood on blocks on a dirt road in the countryside. There was a communal pump down the road where Elvis's mother, Gladys, would go to fetch the water for the family, the chickens in the yard and the outside toilet. Gladys would work picking cotton with baby Elvis

lying beside her; when he grew older he helped her. His father, Vernon, spent time in a penitentiary, a work farm near the Mississippi River, where he'd landed after getting drunk and forging a check.

Not long after, Gladys was evicted from her home when she was unable to pay the monthly twelve-dollar rent, and she and Elvis found themselves living with relatives on welfare until Vernon was released and Elvis's parents were able to rent another house – one of thirteen that Elvis could remember living in during his young life. Vernon's inability to keep a job for long didn't help, nor did his willingness to borrow money to get by, leaving Gladys to struggle to repay all debts and all bills as best she could. They were poor, it's true, but Elvis remembered always having food to eat – although it was sometimes a close call.

But there was always music to help them forget; and religion, often combined. Vernon and Gladys, who had a good voice, would sing as they moved around the house, hymns mostly, and Elvis would join in; and hymns, and later gospel songs, would remain central to his music throughout his life. The style of the service in the church they attended was borrowed from the black gospel singers and preachers, and the uplifting effect of a rousing, physical show on the congregation did not go unremarked by the young Elvis.

Neither did his mother's anxious attention to her boy. Having lost one child she was extra vigilant of the other, and spankings were as much an expression of her fear of loss as they were a form of punishment. But without money

11

Two year old Elvis Presley poses for a family portrait with his parents Vernon Presley and Gladys Presley in 1937 in Tupelo, Mississippi

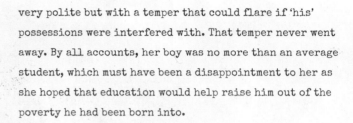

Elvis & parents outside of their home in Tupelo, Mississippi

12

very polite but with a temper that could flare if 'his' possessions were interfered with. That temper never went away. By all accounts, her boy was no more than an average student, which must have been a disappointment to her as she hoped that education would help raise him out of the poverty he had been born into.

Singing continued to be part of his life, and he took a major leap forward along his future path when, at the age of ten, his teacher heard him singing in morning prayer assembly and encouraged him to enter the Mississippi-Alabama Fair and Dairy Show held in Tupelo on October the 3rd 1945. Dressed in cowboy attire and standing on a chair to reach the microphone, he gave his best in 'Old Shep' and came in fifth – or perhaps second, no one can really remember. More importantly, it was his first taste of public performance and its potential rewards; he was given a free ride in the fairground.

When his birthday came around, he was given a guitar as a present. Gladys had thought of the idea, thinking that it would encourage him to sing – and the bike he wanted was too expensive anyway. With help from his mother and the local pastor, his little fingers soon found their way over the fretboard – but no one felt the tremor that occurred in the musical universe; a star had begun his first tentative steps towards fame. From then on, teaching himself mostly, Elvis and his guitar were firm friends.

Although shy about singing in public, he would sometimes face the fear and perform 'Old Shep' again at the local radio station amateur afternoons, on one memorable occasion even accompanied by a country singer of the time, Mississippi Slim.

But the glory was fleeting and poverty caught up with him again. Short of money once more, his parents were forced to move into Tupelo, to the edge of an area of shanties and shacks, where the young Elvis was conspicuous in his jean

for doctors, childhood illnesses were times of special worry and when prayers were the only remedy available, it seemed that God, too, thought her boy was special, because He kept him alive.

Generally he was a good boy, knew that his mother would suffer if he wasn't and tried to stay on the right side of her and God. As, indeed, he did all his life, producing a conflict in later years that all God-fearing showbiz personalities are confronted with and mostly fail to resolve satisfactorily for themselves – favouring the showbiz lifestyle over religious rules.

Elvis attended his first school at East Tupelo Consolidated in 1942; His mother's cosseting had formed a shy child, overalls; a flag of poverty, the sight of which resonated with him even when he was wealthy beyond dreams.

Despite the move and the change of school in 1946 to Milan Junior High, money was still a scarce commodity around the boy now regarded as a loner, and who had developed a stammer on words beginning with the letter 'w' when he became nervous. He would never quite lose it. His pleasures came in the form of the Saturday serial cowboy movies – although his father told him to keep that to himself, it was considered sinful in some quarters – and the comic books at the local library, where Gladys had registered him. And, of course, music and his guitar, which he would take to school regularly. And school did hold one small miracle; Mississippi Slim's son, who was a classmate, and he took the boy who was crazy about music to see his father's radio shows. And joy of joys, Slim offered the 12-year old two slots on his shows, one of which Elvis couldn't

fulfill; he was in the grip of stage fright.

Vernon had been trying to make ends meet again working as a truck driver, but managed to get himself fired once more – he'd been caught making moonshine. It was the trigger for another move, but it was a serendipitous one that within a few years would make the young boy's world turn from grey to multi-coloured.

The family gave away what possessions they had that would not fit into the trunk and inside the 1937 Plymouth. Elvis and his grandma were loaded up, and practically without a cent to their name, they headed off for a new life. It was November 1948. Elvis Presley was 14 years old.

Their destination was Memphis, Tennessee.

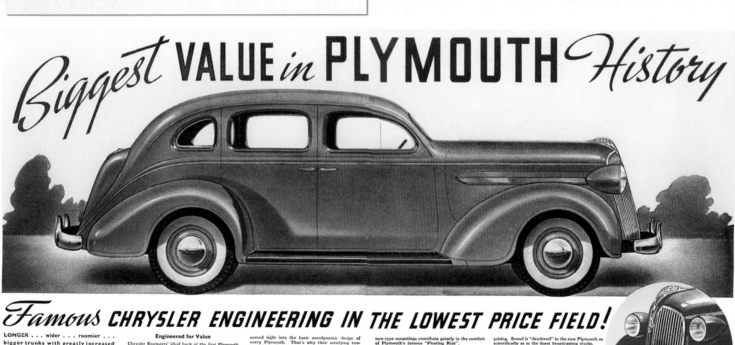

"I THINK I'M GONNA LIKE IT HERE"

There was undoubtedly a sense of a vibrant new beginning for young Elvis; how could it be otherwise in a new city, even though, at first, it was experienced from the rooms of several boarding houses with shared bathrooms and just one hotplate in one room in which they cooked, ate and slept. There was hope, too, when both Vernon and Gladys found new work, which may have lessened her initial loneliness in her new surroundings. As did the arrival of her brother and his wife a little later. Elvis, on the other hand, soon felt at home. And the sense of a new direction for his life must have been increased when they took up residence in a Memphis housing project; their own bathroom, their own sitting room, their own kitchen, and their own two bedrooms.

But more important in forming the man who would become a legend was the proximity to the black area of central Memphis, where Elvis could hear more of the "*... real low down Mississippi singers*" embracing the rhythm and blues that he liked.

His new school, not far from where he now lived, was Humes High School, and although his, slightly excessive, politeness was well-received by his teachers, his fellow schoolmates mocked his country way of talking, dubbing him "*teacher's pet*". But his was the way of ordinary folk who found themselves at the bottom of the social status pyramid; that's what he was and that, at heart, was what he would always remain. He spent a great deal of time not paying attention in class, preferring to daydream about stardom and some of his heroes such as Marlon Brando and Tony Curtis.

But Elvis was not a loner; he would hang about the streets and the house with friends, some of them girls. But singing was still the driving force of his life, and the gospel group harmonies in the revivalist meetings his parents sometimes attended thrilled him, and with his guitar as his best friend – although he was the first to admit in later years that he was a simple rhythm player leaving the complicated guitar work to more skilled hands – he sat in the house playing and singing all through the uncertain period when his voice was breaking, berated by neighbours and his father, but always encouraged by Gladys.

He managed his schoolwork in his own fashion; it was hard to ignore those gorgeous harmonies emanating from the radio and those entrancing lyrics. At least he could now afford to buy a record or two, especially as he supplemented the family income by offering to cut neighbours lawns with his father's new lawnmower. As an adult, Elvis never parted from his old records; they seemed to offer him the comfort of the past as his life became an untameable spiral of hurt.

14

Not many years later, he would find a job in the local movie theatre which meant that he could afford to visit the movie theatres twice a week and, of course, buy himself some sharp clothes in the shops that he favoured because they were frequented by black musicians.

Gradually, Elvis began to find his feet; he let his hair grow longer, formed it into a quiff and added sideburns as soon as he could. Even at that early stage, Elvis was not afraid to stand out from the crowd. A stance that was not without the danger of attracting fearful thuggery; which was where his friend from the football team, Red West saved him. No one wanted to antagonise Red.

So life at school moved forward slowly and uneventfully – until Elvis sang at the annual school minstrel show, for which he had been entered by his perceptive class teacher, Mildred Scrivener. He sang 'Till I Waltz Again with You', and excitedly nonplussed, discovered that his peers liked what he did.

"*It was*", he said, "*amazing how popular I became after that*". It was his first taste of the heady nectar of adulation. His schoolmates' attitude towards him changed as he entered the final months of his school career.

And then school life was over. It was the 3rd of June 1953, and having daydreamed or not, Elvis graduated from high school, the first in his family ever to do so. It was a proud night for both mother and son.

But what now for a poor boy from Memphis? Not college, though he would have liked to have gone on to further education. Then, as now, money was the big American divider. So. The police? The uniform was attractive. Singing in a gospel group appealed to him enormously, too, but the Songfellows singers didn't seem to need him because, as they commented on his audition, he couldn't sing harmony.

But the imperative was to earn money as soon as possible, and so he joined the queues at the local welfare office.

His first job saw him standing at an assembly line. That didn't last more than a few weeks, and he opted to join Crown Electric as an apprentice electrician. $3 an hour. A steady job. Gladys was pleased. Elvis sincerely wanted to do well, rolled his sleeves up and got down to work.

Elvis was magnetically attracted to the Memphis Recording Service owned by Sam Phillips, who was setting up a new label under the name of Sun. Elvis also knew that you could walk in off the street to make a private recording in the offices on Union Avenue. Which, after several false starts due to shyness, is what he bravely did. He chose 'My Happiness' and 'That's When Your Heartaches Begin' for the two sides of his ten-inch acetate disc. Which cost him $3.98 plus tax – and made his mother inordinately proud.

What Elvis didn't know, however, was that the lady at the recording studio, Marion Keisker, had liked what she had heard and had secretly recorded him, to play back to Mr. Phillips when he returned later. He was, she noted down, a good ballad singer.

Marion Keisker was about to give Elvis Presley to the world.

There was another pleasure to add to Elvis's life at this time; the 15-year-old Dixie Locke. She was willing, but it took Elvis a few weeks to prove to her parents, despite her tears and his rather outlandish appearance, that he was a good boy at heart. And they eventually relented. The two could soon be seen together in the movies and listening to the local jukeboxes and even gospel groups – and although the segregation laws meant that they couldn't actually enter the church, they could stand and listen off to the side.

In the meantime, his ambition to become a professional singer burned inside him, and whatever shyness he retained he overcame to drop into the Sun Studio and into nightclubs and other venues around town seeking work as a singer. Without much success; which didn't seem to surprise his father Vernon. Perhaps that even pleased him.

The gods of music, however, had decided not to toy with their protégé for too long. In June 1954, Marion Keisker from Sun Records phoned him. Could he come over that afternoon?

He moved faster than the Roadrunner.

Marion believed in Elvis and had she not pressed Sam Phillips about him, the meteoric rise of Elvis Presley may never have happened. Elvis himself always acknowledged that.

Elvis was to sing a new song that Phillips had been given, 'Without You', which he performed in every style he knew; but Phillips kept asking him to sing it again as he sat watching an unnerved Elvis for the best part of three hours, concentrating listening, wondering.

And then, with faint praise from Philips, it was over. Elvis left the studio in a state that can hardly be described as buoyant.

Not long after that deflation, Elvis was in the movie theatre where his mother brought him some heart-stopping news; guitarist Scotty Moore had been trying to contact him. Mr. Phillips wanted him back in the studio for another audition.

Who was 'Scotty' Moore? Elvis didn't know. It didn't matter, either. Fortunately, he didn't know that the guitarist's first reaction on hearing the young man's name had been, *"His name – Elvis Presley – what kind of a name is that?"*

So, blissfully unaware, Elvis went over to the guitarist's house, where the two chatted and went through a few songs, and Moore tried not to be blinded by the young man's pink trousers and lacy shirt.

"But he'd play along, and when he didn't know the chords he'd just keep playing, keep singing. And this went on for a couple of hours", recalled Scotty in an interview years later.

That night, the two men, together with double bass player Bill Black, got down to work in Sun Studios.

Phillips listened as Elvis sang; 'Harbour Lights' or 'I Love you Because', but all Elvis got by way of encouragement was *"That's fine"*. Not very encouraging; but what did Philips want from him?

They took a break, and Elvis, by now as tense as a tightly wound spring with the fear of imminent failure, sang to himself; 'That's All Right'. Bill and Scotty joined in, jamming for the fun of it – *"I had never heard the song"* Scottie remembered. *"Bill had never heard it, and I took the guitar and started playing, looking for something; we were just jamming."* – and Sam's voice for the first time sounded out on a positive note; *"It don't sound too bad"*. Such fulsome praise indeed, and it led to the trio rehearsing the song and recording it, with Sam guiding them in the direction he wanted the song to go.

The two experienced musicians knew instinctively that something had happened in the studio that night with this young man. They weren't quite sure what. It was so different; neither fish nor fowl, neither blues nor country, a unique amalgam of both.

Elvis, with the help of his friends, had just created a vibrant new sound of his very own. But would anyone accept it?

It was July 1954. Elvis was 19 years old. His life, and the music world with it, was about to be turned on its head.

17

Elvis Presley, hatted and shirtless, holds a stack of 45's of 'That's All Right, Mama,' his first commercial recording.

"THIS IS LIVING"

Sam Phillips had his friend Dewey Phillips play the song on Dewey's 'Red, Hot, and Blue' radio show. The DJ played the song eleven times, and the calls came in thick and fast. Dewey called Elvis in for a live interview. Cleverly, he didn't tell the terrified young man that he was already on air. By next day, the orders for the record were already coming in. Which was wonderful.

Except that there was no 'B' side.

Back into the studio went the three boys.

'Blue Moon of Kentucky' was a country song. But by the time Phillips had ramped up the pace and Elvis had worked his vocal magic, it certainly wasn't going to please the country crowd anymore.

But the record played all over Memphis; and as it turned out, both the blues boys and the country boys were happy with what they heard. It soon reached number three in the local charts. Elvis watched people buy his record in town and experienced a thrill like no other.

Sam suggested they form a legal trio with Scotty as manager. Scotty, fair to Elvis in a way very few people would be subsequently, insisted the singer get 50% as his cut. Which at that moment was 50% of precisely nothing.

Just a short time later, the three were booked to play in the afternoon at the Memphis Overton Park Shell amphitheatre as part of a programme featuring yodeler Slim Whitman. Faced with such illustrious company, Elvis was trembling like a man waiting for execution.

Then they were on. Bill set the rhythm, and Elvis came in over the top of it with 'That's All Right', focusing on his job – until he became uncomfortably aware of an increasingly loud and wild noise in the audience. Unnerved, as soon as they had left the stage he asked Sam what was happening. Sam didn't quite know himself... but he did know that it meant the crowd liked his band, so he sent them out again ... and the reaction was even wilder from the females out front. Scotty later reckoned that it was the fact that Elvis was moving his legs to the rhythm that had got the girls fired up. Even Whitman noticed it. Elvis had been given his first lesson in how to work an audience. And from that day on, he worked hard at his homework. *"I'm not trying to be sexy"*, he once said. *"It's just my way of expressing myself when I move around."* What happened to his female fans when he expressed himself was something of which he was very well aware.

Once he was in control of the effects, he loved the attention. He would flirt with his audiences, his legs jack-knifing. And those flirts led to other activities off stage. He didn't tell that to Dixie; but she had her quiet worries about the adulation. Neither were the 'flirts' entirely without danger; a first encounter with the irate – and jealous – male partner of an over-excited woman ended when the soldier knocked him down some stairs

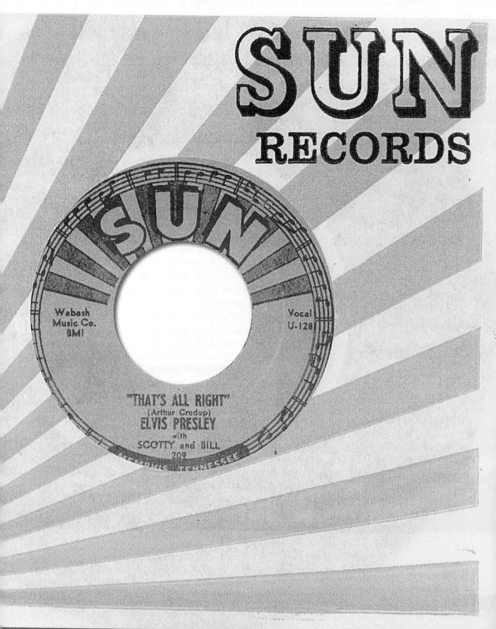

SUN RECORDS

Wabash Music Co. BMI

Vocal U-128

"THAT'S ALL RIGHT"
(Arthur Crudup)
ELVIS PRESLEY
with SCOTTY and BILL
209

that was inside his memory, put there by the R&B and doo-wop records he used to buy. There was a new guitar, too, as he had a little more cash in his hands; a Martin D-18 for $175, an extravagance he had never been able to contemplate in the past. And even more exciting in a year that was uncovering treasures unheard of was the introduction to B. B. King.

Throughout 1954 and '55, the bookings slowly grew in number. The boys drove and slept in the car on their way to small-scale venues; but the ball was rolling and their songs were now being sold in other states, too. Most musicians of the era would take Benzedrine to help them get through the gruelling days of travelling and performances. And Elvis's energetic routines needed to

7" of That's All Right, first single on Sun Records

after a gig one night. Scotty and Bill would never let him go anywhere alone after that.

Life began to change. Between visits to Dixie, Elvis would rehearse with Scotty, use the Sun Studio as an experimental playground or play gigs at the Eagle's Nest, a nightclub just outside Memphis. Elvis tried out many styles of vocal delivery, the wistful, the pleading, the gentle balladic, drawing on the deep well of knowledge

Elvis with guitar player Scotty Moore left and bass player Bill Black on 'Louisiana Hayride', October 16, 1954

L-R Elvis Presley, Bill Black, Scotty Moore, Sam Phillips, in Sun Records studio

Elvis Presley in 1955

20

be maintained somehow. Nonetheless, for Elvis it was a period of enchantment that he would always remember with happiness, recalled whenever he sang 'That's All Right', which he did on stage for the rest of his life.

It did not take long for the ambitious Sam to fulfill a dream for the trio; an appearance at Grand Ole Opry in Nashville for a radio show. They felt as though they were rocketing up to the moon.

They went skidding downhill with the hillbilly audience faster than a sack of dropped potatoes, and some nondescript, self-important manager told Elvis not to give up his job as a truck driver. That hurt. So much, that Elvis never went back there ever again.

Ignoring the malicious advice, Elvis and the boys all gave up their day jobs, Scotty and Bill now rejoicing in the name of the Blue Moon Boys. Which meant that they had

to be focused on producing new material. Unfortunately, none of them could write songs. So they had to rummage through old long-forgotten ones that they could vamp up. Out of the pile rose 'Milk Cow Blues' to become their third single after 'Good Rockin' Tonight'.

By the early months of 1955, when Scotty had decided to relinquish the manager role, Elvis and the trio were becoming minor regional celebrities, especially thanks to their appearance on the Louisiana Hayride show for which Presley had been engaged for a year of Saturday-night performances. The house drummer, D. J. Fontana, was added to give an extra dimension to the trio. Fontana, who then became a fixture of Elvis's backing band, recalled those early years; "*Well, his voice was so unusual for that time period and his clothes were unusual – his dress with the peg pants and all that stuff and stripes down his pants leg. And he was a good-looking kid, a good-looking guy, and I said, "Hey this guy might do ok – who knows?"* he had that certain charisma about him that there was no way for him to miss, no way".

Gradually, Presley's indeterminate style, which would later be dubbed 'Rockabilly', led to him trailing a list of descriptive names in his wake, such as *"The Memphis Flash"*, *"The King of Western Bop"* or *"The Hillbilly Cat"*.

As his singing began to bring in plaudits for him, fame started to curl her seductive tentacles around Elvis, who was now recognised as he walked down the street in Memphis. Without realising it had happened, he was the de facto leader of the band, choosing the set sequences and the songs. Bill and Scotty, wisely understanding where the root of their newfound recognition was planted, deferred to him in all things. Not that it stopped Bill from performing acrobatics with his base, while Elvis jerked and twisted at the front of the stage. Which

brought in complaints from parents that what he did was *"dirty"*. Elvis would always reply the same way; *"Rock and roll music, if you like it, you can't help but to move to it. That's what happens to me. I can't help it."*

Elvis was learning how important it was to be a showman, just as Sinatra had learned before him, and like Sinatra, Elvis worked on finding ways to give his fans what they wanted, performing to the best of his ability for them. Whatever nerves afflicted him backstage, on stage he was buoyed by the energy and goodwill of his audience, and he gave it back to them, to his *"friends"*, as he called them, in fistfuls.

His style began to infiltrate other bands, too, and unknown to the man who caused it, as the Elvis effect gradually rippled outwards, it washed towards a man who Presley credited with making him the star he became.

Elvis Presley preforms on stage with his back up singers 'The Jordanaires' in 1955

ELVIS PRESLEY IS TOLD: 'CLEAN IT UP'

ELVIS ("The Pelvis") PRESLEY has been given police orders to clean up his show.

Parents complained about his Hollywood show on Tuesday night —when there were many children in the audience.

Presley was said to have "wiggled like a striptease artist."

And yesterday Hollywood's vice squad was ordered to see that Presley cuts out any "sexy overtones" from his performance.

MEMORIAL AUDITORIUM
BUFFALO, NY. ★ 8:00 P.M.
SAT., JAN. 21 - 1956

ELVIS
PRESLEY   JORDANAIRES
"Tickets $1.75 - All Seats Reserved"

22

IN
P
A
MULTNOM
MON., SEPT.
$ 1⁵⁰ – $
TICKET
J. K.
S. W. 5 th

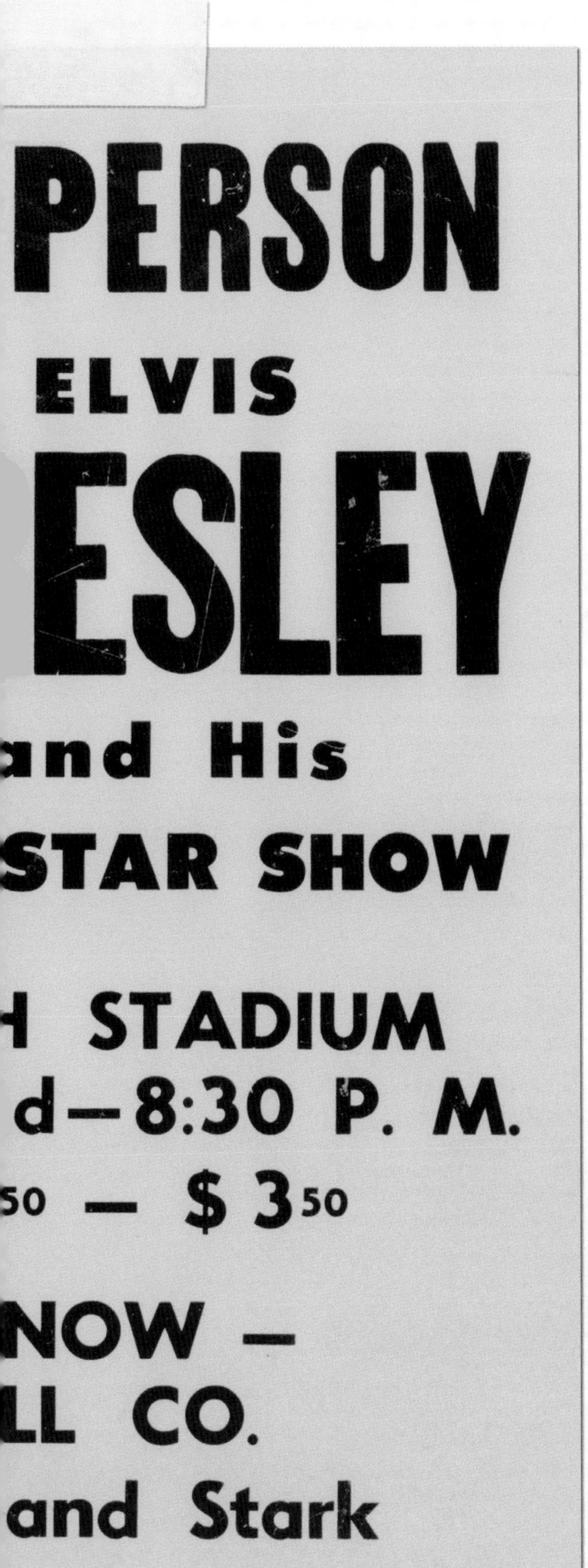

PERSON

ELVIS

ESLEY

and His

STAR SHOW

H STADIUM

d—8:30 P. M.

50 — $3⁵⁰

NOW —

LL CO.

and Stark

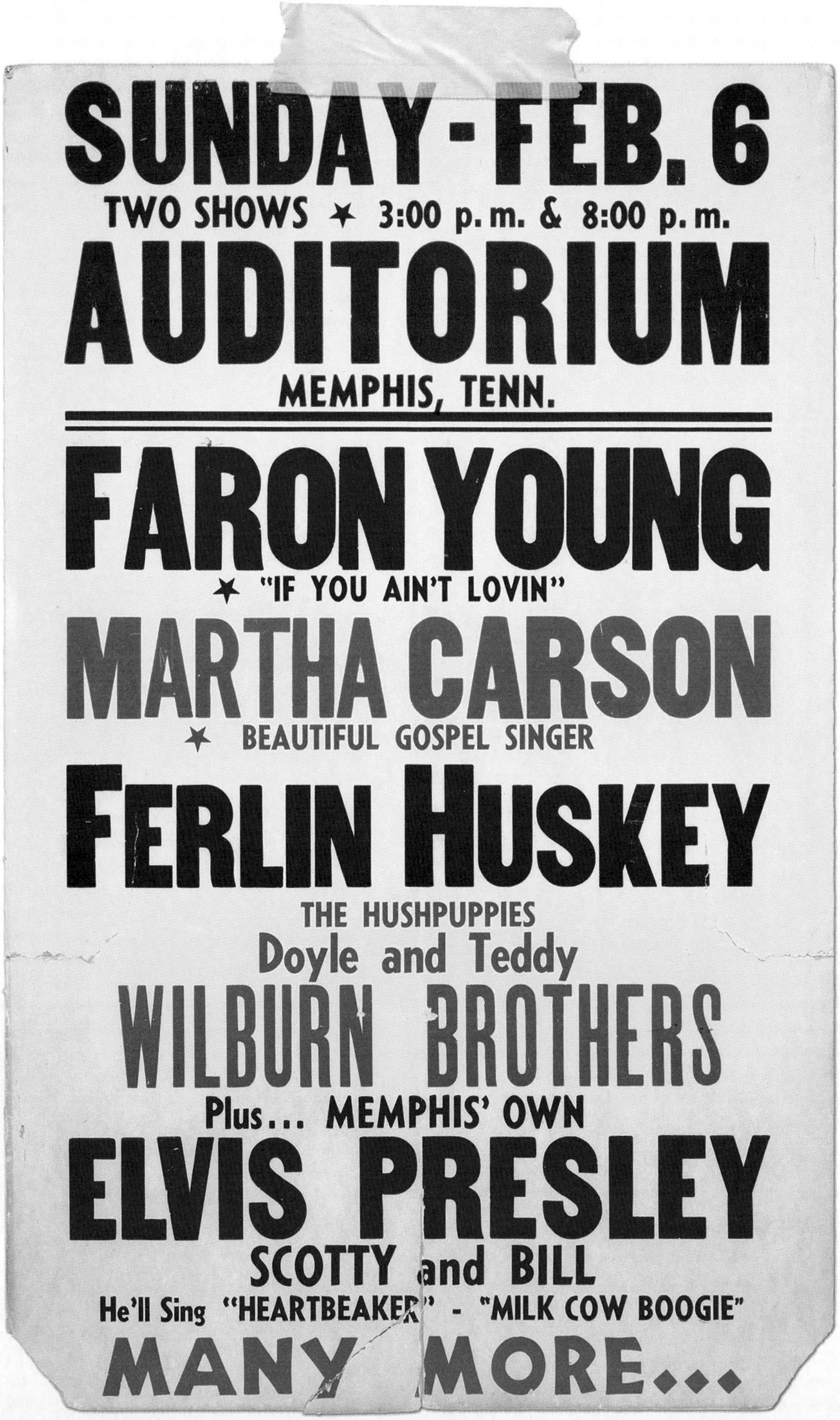

SUNDAY - FEB. 6
TWO SHOWS ★ 3:00 p.m. & 8:00 p.m.
AUDITORIUM
MEMPHIS, TENN.

FARON YOUNG
★ "IF YOU AIN'T LOVIN"
MARTHA CARSON
★ BEAUTIFUL GOSPEL SINGER
FERLIN HUSKEY
THE HUSHPUPPIES
Doyle and Teddy
WILBURN BROTHERS
Plus... MEMPHIS' OWN
ELVIS PRESLEY
SCOTTY and BILL
He'll Sing "HEARTBEAKER" - "MILK COW BOOGIE"
MANY MORE...

23

Colonel Tom Parker was a Dutch-born American manager. He was in his forties when Elvis met him for the first time. Parker didn't know music from a barrel of beer went the sneering. Maybe not. But he was savvy enough to recognise a new trend, and although Presley never warmed to him and would always think of Parker as the blunt, ungainly man who brought him in the dollars, by the summer of 1955, Parker had metamorphosed into Presley's *"special advisor"*. Memphis radio personality Bob Neal was Presley's manager at that point in time.

In the blink of an eye, the trio were out on a Hank Snow Tour for Jamboree Attractions, the company run by the Colonel - Elvis would always call him that - and country singer Hank Snow, with venues and audiences of sizes that they could only have dreamt of until then. And proper pay days. Elvis received his first advance of $425. An advance! Which helped to paper over the fact that the Colonel was trying to edge out Scotty and Bill, finally managing to get them put on salary instead of taking a percentage of the earnings. As far as the Colonel was concerned, there was only one man he was interested in and that was Elvis. Completely misunderstanding that the boys helped Elvis to produce that magical sound that Parker understood and loved to the exclusion of all else; the sound of money. And he understood how to make Elvis feel eternally grateful... very useful when the Colonel later came to squeeze more and more money from his star.

And the Colonel had been busy on another front, too, trying to buy Elvis's contract with Sam Phillips. He finally succeeded, of course, although Sam gave in reluctantly and was paid $35,000, a huge sum for those days. Which also came in very handy for the cash-strapped entrepreneur. Still, Sam was wistful about

saying goodbye to their time together, their work; Sam had Elvis's interests at heart. Not many people would from now on. Sam assured Elvis that he could come and talk to him at any time. Elvis's part of the deal saw him take a 5% royalty and a $5500 dollar cash advance. His apprenticeship was over. The singer was now a protégé of one of the world's largest record companies; RCA.

And there were plans to set up a publishing company with the singer as a co-owner, from which Elvis stood to make vast amounts of money. Unaware, gripped by the excitement of a glittering future, Elvis was slowly being formed into a money-making machine for others; there would be no room for sentiment or personal discomfort, no understanding of artistic sensibility.

Parker, of course, had told no one, and he had Vernon sign the contract, because Elvis was still a minor, coming away with his own huge chunk of the deal. And Parker's partner, Hank Snow? Hank had been slipped a musical Mickey Finn. Hank Snow was yesterday.

Whilst Elvis was clambering up the ladder of stardom, back home there was some difficult emotional news waiting for him. Dixie was dating another boy. Hardly surprising, but the news still devastated Elvis, and she retained a place in his heart for a long time to come. Deep down, however, he understood and accepted; his life was moving quickly in a very different direction from those in down home Memphis. And as far as girls were concerned? Well - he was 20 years old, and there wasn't exactly a shortage, was there?

Life was good and getting even better.

EAGLES NEST

IN PERSON
MEMPHIS OWN...

ELVIS PRESLEY

WITH SCOTTY & BILL

♪ ♫ SINGING ♪ ♫

"HEART BREAKER" *"THATS ALL RIGHT"*
"GOOD ROCKIN"

AS HEARD ON...

WHBQ

M.C. DEWEY PHILLIPS

EXTRA ORDINARY MPHS D.J.

25

Elvis Presley with his manager
Colonel Tom Parker pose in front of
a picture of the RCA Victor dog in
circa 1957 in Memphis, Tennessee

Elvis Presley 1954 Eagles Nest Original Hand-Painted
Concert Poster, Memphis TN

"SHAKE, RATTLE & ROLL"

Elvis's old school friend Red West was often his driver now, because Scotty, Bill and drummer D. J. had been relegated to another vehicle; it was good to have Red to talk to about life, a man who was not involved in the music world. Red was also useful as a bodyguard. Because although no one in Memphis bothered him with more than a smile of recognition, the female fans and their mostly irate boyfriends were not so considerate. The touring schedule was intense, and there were many occasions, especially in Texas, when Elvis needed police protection. "It was almost frightening, the reaction that came to Elvis from the teenaged boys. So many of them, through some sort of jealousy, would practically hate him... they'd get a gang and try to waylay him or something", his manager Bob Neal recalled.

In January of 1956, Elvis and the band arrived in Nashville to start recording for his first album with RCA. The RCA executives were nervous, and Elvis discovered that he was going to backed by more than a three piece; Chet Atkins, pianist Floyd Cramer, and the Jordanaires quartet were there, too. With three microphones to catch his vocals when he moved around, Elvis sang the Carl Perkins' hit that was to become something of a signature song for him; "Blue Suede Shoes".

"Heartbreak Hotel" had been co-written by Tommy Durden and Mae Boren Axton, who became known as the "Queen Mother of Nashville" with some 200 songs to her credit. Elvis had met her in Florida when she was a publicist, and she had introduced Parker to the singer. Although he recorded it, no one else liked the song much; they found it too gloomy –

except Elvis, whose sharp ears knew what the song was worth. It didn't make it onto the album. But as a single the song topped Billboard's Top 100 chart for seven weeks. Parker had arranged for Elvis to make his first appearance on coast-to-coast TV with CBS and Jacky Gleason's Stage Show, hosted by the Dorsey brothers; but the show was not doing so well and no one in New York knew Elvis, so the theatre was half empty. Not that it mattered; he had earned another $1250. And there was to be a second bite at the cherry the following week.

26

Presley portrait in 1956 in Memphis, Tennessee

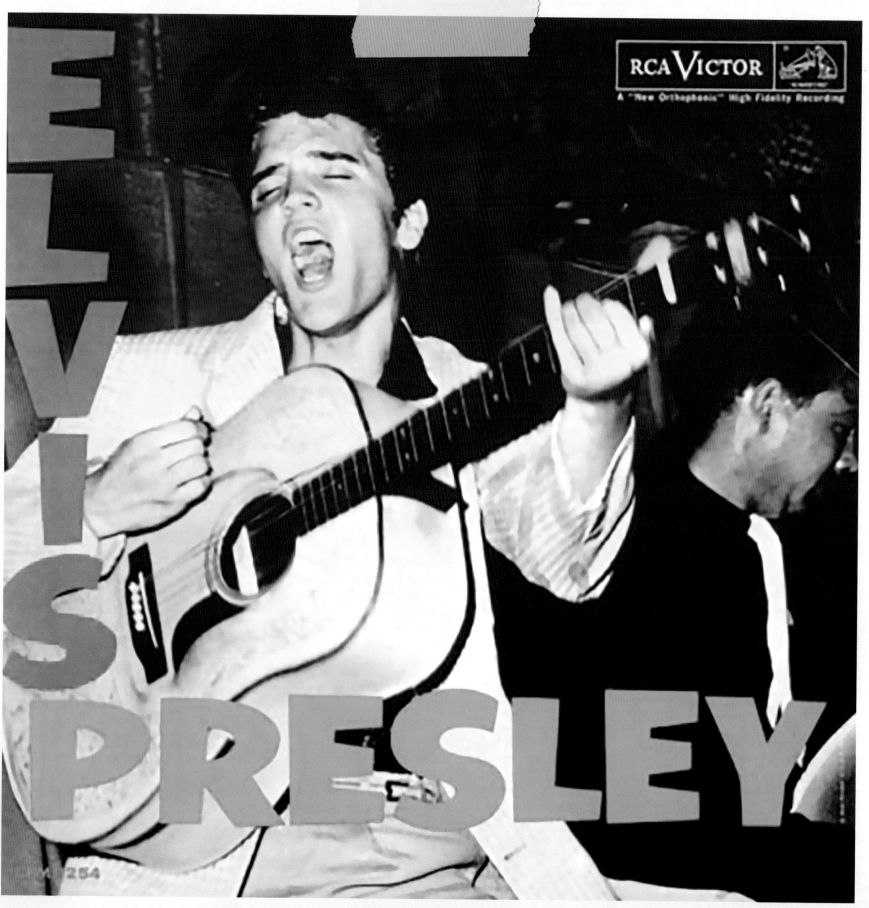

27

Cover of first album

Elvis Sings; Wows 15,000

BY CHARLES MANOS
Free Press Staff Writer

Elvis Presley, the rock-n-roll dreamboat, danced up a storm in Detroit Friday.

Some 15,000 teen-agers, mostly girls, paid nearly $25,000 in small change to watch him sing, play the guitar and wiggle across the stage at the Fox Theater.

His take-home pay for three performances was estimated at $10,000.

* * *

TIRED and yawning between performances, the 21-year-old hillbilly blues singer said he is as amazed as anyone over his tremendous success.

In less than six months, bobby-soxers have bought more than five million recordings by the former truck driver from Memphis, Tenn.

A modest, good-looking youth who does not drink or smoke, Presley described it all as a "dream come true."

"I never was a lady killer in high school," he said. "I had my share of dates—but that's all."

Wearing long smooth sideburns and a bright red satin shirt, Presley said he wished he had the time to have a coke with each one of his fans.

* * *

"**I'D LIKE** to take 'em all for a ride in my new car," he said.

He owns four Cadillacs.

Ernestine Waynick, 14, of 428 Heidt, was typical of the teen-agers in the audience.

"Wow," she said. "I like his actions."

She said she ran errands and turned in pop-bottles to save $4.50.

That's the price for the three performances.

28

Presley. His name, written large in lurid pink and green, was emblazoned over a picture of Elvis with guitar, his mouth open like the Liverpool Mersey Tunnel. It was designed to catch attention, which it did. To Parker's delight.

The Elvis effect struck CBS, too. For the second show, he regaled his TV audience with 'Baby, Let's Play House' and 'Tutti Frutti'. Tickets for Gleason's Stage Show were now being snapped up, and Elvis was rebooked, Gleason adding four more performances. The CBS grey suits even relented and let him sing 'Heartbreak Hotel'. He had to fit the TV appearances into a tight touring schedule that took him away for three weeks along the east coast, playing four shows a day on occasion, accompanied by the now familiar sound of fans screaming. That scream meant that Elvis

Elvis bounded on and launched into "Shake, Rattle and Roll", keeping the shaking down to acceptable limits as he had been asked to do – but his performance still jammed the phone lines at CBS with complaints. However, Gleason liked him. So much that he had Elvis also sing "I Got a Woman".

Back in the studio once more, Elvis recorded the last of his eight songs for the album – to be called, simply, Elvis

Presley portrait in 1956 in Memphis, Tennessee

was beginning to acquire a whole team of people to manage his life; including his father, Vernon, who gave up his job to take care of all the things Parker didn't, including the increasing piles of fan mail. That scream also meant a new seven-room house for his parents and himself on Audubon Drive in 1956, though it would be a short stay. Fans and the media soon began to arrive there in increasing numbers, and even the most understanding neighbours were getting restless. Something would have to give.

As March drew to a close, Elvis's orphan child, 'Heartbreak Hotel', released in January, had defied RCA's predictions and was rising up the charts. And now Hollywood beckoned. It was the start of a dream come true for Elvis. But before he went to join the celluloid stars, he had other singing commitments; appearances on the Milton Berle Show and a two-week stint in Las Vegas were coming up.

Performing on the Milton Berle Show, singing 'Hound Dog' on the second occasion, led to another TV slot – on the Steve Allen Show, where Presley would be humiliated, being allowed to play for less than one minute and appearing with a Bassett hound in a top hat and bow tie. Elvis would say that the Allen show had been the most ridiculous performance of his career. He did it so as not to tarnish his image, because by now he was being vilified in no uncertain terms; "lewd", "vulgar", "obscene" and "morally degenerate" were just some of the pejoratives, "suggestive" being the least offensive. The worst was possibly, "Presley is a definite danger to the security of the United States", which was intoned by J. Edgar Hoover. Also, the phrase "Elvis the Pelvis" was doing the rounds, an expression which he loathed and called "one of the most childish" he had ever

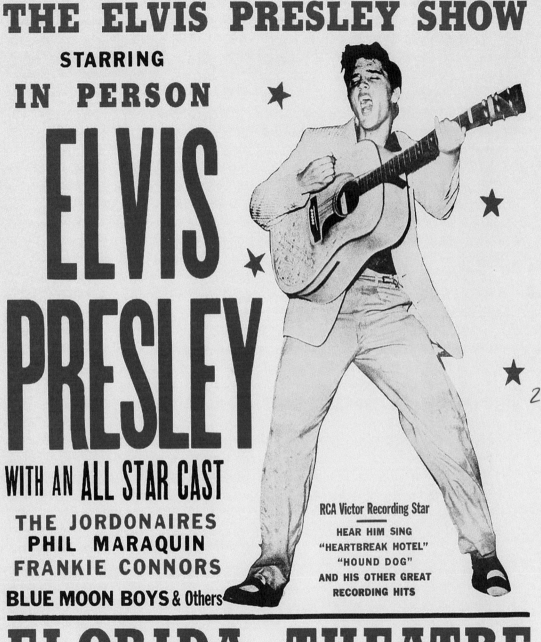

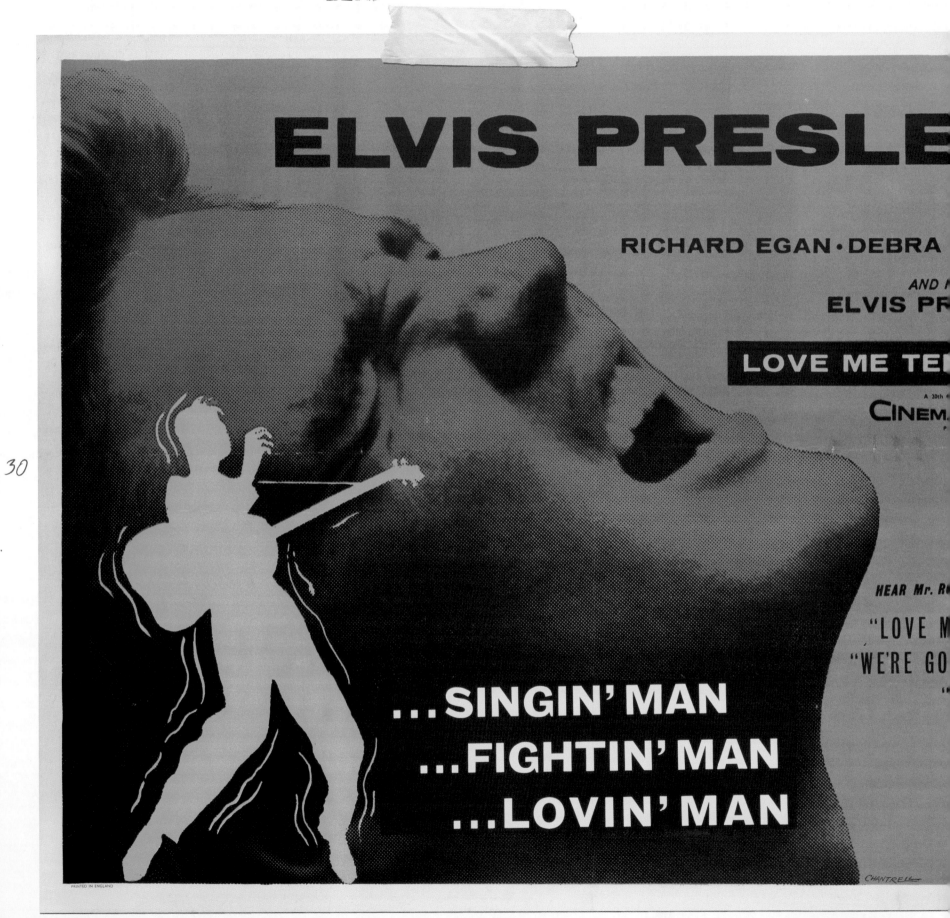

A poster for Robert D. Webb's 1956 drama 'Love Me Tender' starring Elvis Presley

IN PERSON!

ELVIS PRESLEY SHOW

N° 3566

CHARLOTTE COLISEUM   CHARLOTTE, N.C.

TUESDAY, JUNE 26, 1956

Show 8:30 p.m.   Doors open 7:00 p.m.

GENERAL ADMISSION TICKET

ADMISSION: IN ADVANCE _____ $1.25
AT DOOR _____ 1.50

Federal State and Local Taxes, if any, included

SHOW RAIN OR SHINE   NO REFUNDS

ELVIS PRESLEY
Sensational new RCA-Victor
Star - In Person

ELVIS PRESLEY SHOW

N° 1541

HOBART ARENA   TROY, OHIO

Saturday, November 24, 1956

THIS TICKET GOOD 3 P.M. SHOW ONLY

SPECIAL ADVANCE SALE ADM. ____ $2.00

Federal, State and local taxes, if any, Included

SHOW RAIN OR SHINE   NO REFUNDS

ELVIS PRESLEY
Sensational new RCA-Victor
Star - In Person

heard coming from an adult. "I don't care what they say", he told one reporter, "it ain't nasty", and he pointed out that the "coloured folks have been singing and playing it just like I do... for more years than I know". Elvis knew a lot about blues and other music genres, often surprising other musicians, who thought he knew little.

One of the Colonel's few false steps in those early years, was to book Elvis into the Las Vegas New Frontier Hotel to play to a middle-aged audience, who didn't know what the young man was up to; and vice versa. But at least his jokes went down well. Elvis had no interest in the other delights offered by Las Vegas, the gambling machines and tables, preferring, at twenty-one years of age, flirting and the dodgems, and although he enjoyed his time there, it would be another thirteen years before he would return to woo an audience far more receptive to the charms of an older man.

But Elvis could afford to ignore the detractors. Fans adored him and 'Hound Dog' and it's "B" side, 'Don't be Cruel', were about to become mega hits, whilst 'Heartbreak Hotel' had climbed to number one in the US charts, Elvis's first.

The speed at which his life was changing, truly did worry Elvis; worry not only about what success might do to him

but that one day that success might simply vanish. "I might be herding sheep next year", he would tell reporters, who would laugh. But Elvis was not laughing. He could see the seductive trappings of success everywhere; in the Cadillacs and Lincolns outside the house and his father's happiness at his extraordinary change in fortune. Gladys, frightened by the hysteria that her son engendered in his female fans, would also complain that the Colonel "...is going to work you to your death. It ain't right". But the dangers were less apparent to Elvis then.

When he had appeared on Jackie Gleason's show, he had received a valuable piece of advice from the older showman; "...you're going to be a very big star..." he told Elvis. "Don't hide, because if you do, you're going to be the loneliest guy in the world". But Elvis was no longer in charge of his own life or able to move too freely, and if he did, he was reprimanded by Parker; Elvis was already the property of the moneymen and the fans. As songwriter Mike Stoller recalled, Presley was 'protected' by his manager and entourage. "He was removed... they kept him separate." Hollywood would only help set the problem in concrete.

And that's where he was headed next.

"DON'T LEAVE ME NOW"

Filming the western Love Me Tender and its musical interludes took up less than three weeks of Elvis's time. As so often, he had to overcome the prejudices of other professionals; his female lead, Debra Paget, for example, pleasantly surprised that he wasn't a moron, apparently.

The schedule wasn't onerous, and there was time to record another album in the evening hours. After all, he had a record number of singles in the Hot Hundred: nine; an achievement previously unheard of, so RCA wanted to capitalise on this huge success and flood the market with Elvis. As usual, new songs were few and far between, so Little Richard and Mike Stoller songs were on the album. And the eponymous title song of the film – the title was changed from The Reno Brothers – was a phenomenal hit, with advance sales topping the million mark, another music industry first.

Although the movie Love Me Tender was released in November, it ended the year of 1956 with a roar as the 23rd highest-grossing film, having recouped its costs within two weeks of release. Amid lukewarm critical response, it's true – leaving Elvis feeling that he had been out of his depth and should not have done the film at all, although some critics gave Elvis's acting talents praise. And praise was what he was now getting from famous TV host Ed Sullivan, who had also changed his opinion of the singer 180 degrees. Something that Elvis was becoming accustomed to, perhaps noting that the warmth of his welcome increased in line with the increased ratings for their shows.

For Elvis, 1956 had been the year he became famous and clocked up one hundred and ninety-one concerts; he was said to be the second most famous American after the president; he was the voice of fifties youth; he was a magnet for the opposite sex; he was wealthy and adored; he was not only the victim of lies and jealous slanders but also of name calling; "White Negro" was one such epithet. His dreams had all turned to reality in vivid Technicolor. There were fans hanging like bunches of grapes outside his house constantly – Gladys used to give them lemonade and let them telephone their parents from the house – and it was becoming impossible to move freely anywhere, as the unknown boy from Memphis had done not so many months before. But the lovely girls were a plus in his crazy life, although with so many in tow, they were not so lovely with each other and there were often sparks of female jealousy.

In defiance of Parker, Elvis popped into Sun Records and sang with Johnny Cash and Carl Perkins and visited an "all Negro talent" show at the local radio station. All part of the vain attempt to remain normal.

Christmas at Audubon Drive with his family helped, but even that semi-retreat was shortly to be replaced by something bigger and less personal.

The problem was that although the fans didn't bother the Presley family, their ever-increasing numbers were causing problems; and not only in the neighbourhood as they blocked streets with the cars in which they sat with the music turned up loud, and camped out and on the front lawns;

the braver fans would also clamber over Presley's garden walls to leave messages on the cars. What was even more distressing was that the neighbours' complaints were aimed more at what they considered to be a lowbrow Mississippi family and their visiting relatives next door than at the fans in the street. Rumours about a petition requesting them to leave the street were already circulating. Elvis knew that he and his family had nothing to be ashamed of, but his mother was upset. It was time to move again. Vernon was instructed to find them something suitable where no one would be upset by their presence. What he found would eventually become a national institution.

So ended 1956, an extraordinary year in which Elvis, having enjoyed more songs in the top 100 than any artist before him, made $22 million in merchandising sales to add to his phenomenal record sales.

1957 brought with it the possibility of being drafted; the probability, in fact. It was as unwelcome to him as to most young men starting out on their careers. Elvis was also about to make his third appearance on the Ed Sullivan Show and earn the rest of his unprecedented $50,000, this time wearing the kind of outlandish costume that was later to become his hallmark; make up on his eyes and what was described as a kind of harem outfit. (One of his girlfriends would give him a gold lamé waistcoat, which he wore on the Ed Sullivan show and which gave him the idea of the gold suit that would make its appearance on his tour in 1957.) With his hair falling over his eyes, his whirling legs were denied to television viewers, because he was filmed only from the waist up. But the screams from the television audience told them what was happening from there on down.

Already shaping up to equal the previous year, three number one hits heralded the start of this new year; 'Too Much', 'All Shook Up' and '(Let Me Be Your) Teddy Bear'. Before he knew it, he was on his way back to Hollywood for his

second film; travelling by train, because Gladys was always afraid when he flew.

Once again, Elvis was going to sing in a movie and once again, it was Jerry Leiber and Mike Stoller who provided a song that gave the film its title; the balladic 'Loving You'. Elvis and the band were allowed to record in a sound studio and not on a soundstage; but the acoustics weren't right for them there, and they were happier improvising with one another uninterrupted until they had found what they wanted.

During the sessions, Elvis met Dudley Brooks a black pianist and Paramount's assistant music director, and from then on Elvis would always have Dudley with him when he was recording in Hollywood. Elvis was treated

Elvis Presley and Johnny Cash pose for a portrait in December of 1957 in Memphis, Tennessee

34

differently from the other actors on a movie set, and was
wary of friendships with his fellow actors, fearing that
it was his fame rather than his character that attracted
them. He felt out of place in their world, rarely attending
film premieres. The Elvis effect always put paid to any
normality that he sought.

Something else that happened – before the shoot – would
also stay with Elvis for the rest of his life; he died his
hair black; it was a suggestion from the Paramount men, and
it would look good in his first Technicolor movie.

Loving You was his first starring role and told the story
of a deliveryman discovered by a publicist and groomed to
become a rock 'n' roll star; the love interest was provided
by 18-year-old Dolores Hart, Mario Lanza's niece. His
parents had come down to Hollywood, and they were even
extras in the scene where he sang 'Got a Lot of Livin' to
Do', fulfilling one of Gladys's childhood dreams. Seeing
them off for the journey home made him sad. Still, there
was a reason to get back to see them as soon as the film was
over, because they'd told him that they had found a house, a
mansion that he might like.

It was eight miles south of Memphis, out in the country, so
no close neighbours to disturb or be disturbed. When Elvis
saw it, he knew he had to live there on that ranch with its
big old oak trees, however dilapidated the house might be.
There was plenty of room; it had seven bedrooms and was
on sale for $102,500. He claimed it with a $1000 deposit
that very day, and from the moment it was his, the property
was in a state of constant flux. Vernon played the role of
estate manager, overseeing the building of the swimming
pool, the hog pen and the chicken coop.

Elvis was a night owl. He had his bedroom, with his specially
made nine-foot square bed painted in dark midnight blue and
matching the curtains designed to keep out the daylight. At
the end of the long, curving driveway, he had electrically

operated iron gates installed, which were embellished with musical notes. His own idea. Who cared what people thought. This place was his; this place was Graceland.

Liberace had never cared about what people thought, and Liberace had taught the singer an important lesson; clothes make the man. People judge you by what you wear; dress expensively, give them spectacle, and they will respect you no matter what. So, on tour that spring of 1957, Elvis wore a gold suit. Maybe a gold Cadillac wouldn't be a bad idea, either. It would match the gold records, of which another one was heading his way for 'All Shook Up'; it had gone to number one in the US and the UK.

Yes, Elvis had become an international star in a frighteningly short space of time. Frightening, too, sometimes, the hysteria that he engendered and the breathlessness of his life; for $250,000 and half of the profits, he was back in Hollywood to film the movie Jailhouse Rock before Loving You had even been released.

Jerry Leiber and Mike Stoller were back on board writing four songs for the movie, and as they were producers as well, Elvis enjoyed talking to them. They also wrote him a love song; 'Don't'. Which got him into trouble with the Colonel; for not telling him about it. Lost revenue. When the Colonel began to rant and make Elvis feel ungrateful, the singer remained silent.

Jailhouse Rock had the dubious honour of seeing Elvis quit the set for his hotel room after his backing group, the

Elvis Presley on the set of Jailhouse Rock, directed by Richard Thorpe

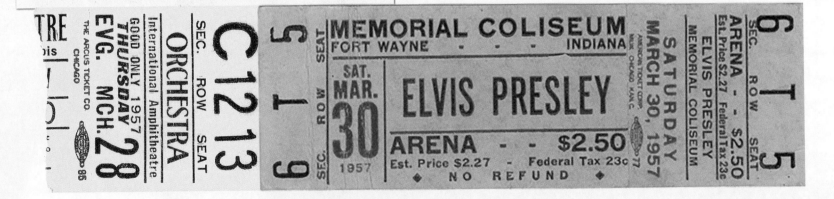

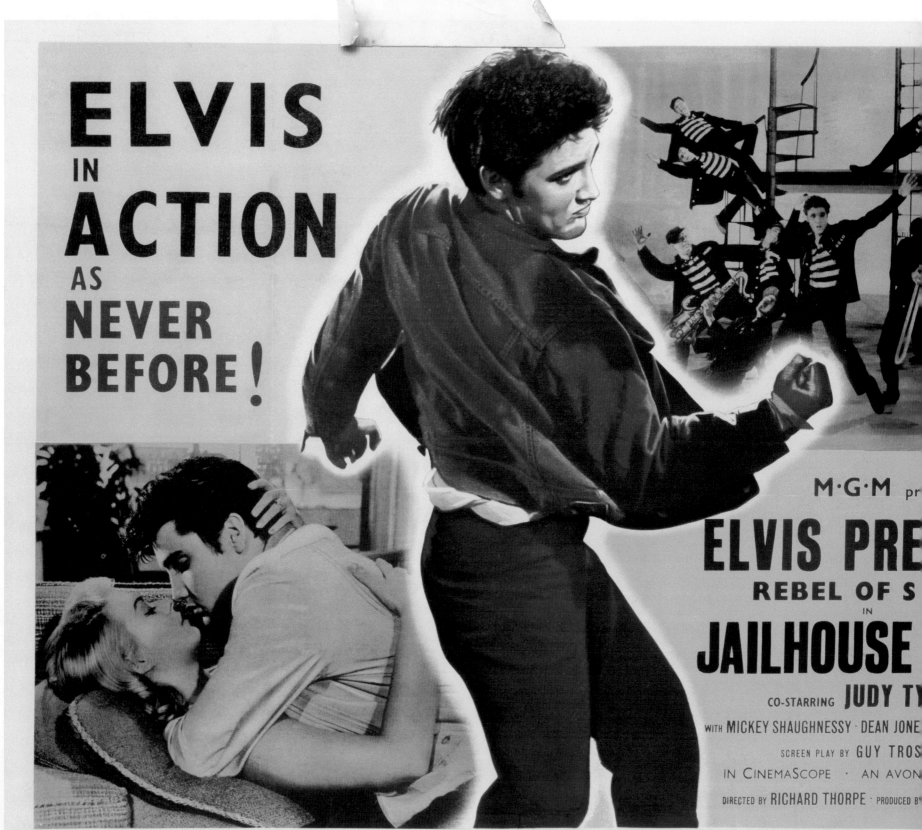

36

Movie poster for *Jailhouse Rock*

Elvis Presley on the set of Jailhouse Rock, directed by Richard Thorpe

Jordanaires, had been forbidden to rehearse with him. Now he felt confident enough of his own value not to allow himself to be pushed around by everyone. It took two days for him to calm down. After that, the MGM executives left him alone.

Elvis's anger outburst to his cousins that day, justified as it might have been, was not an isolated incident. Jealousy wasn't confined to his girlfriends; he, too, was often subjected to its whiplash, and it cracked one day when the Jordanaires had been singing background vocals with someone else, which they were contractually allowed to do. But one of their records, Tab Hunter's version of 'Young Love', had toppled Elvis from the number one position on the charts, and he raged, hurling accusations of disloyalty around.

Neither was the apparent bond between Scotty, Bill and Elvis all that it had once been. Scotty and Bill now inhabited a parallel, less glorified world in comparison to their front man, staying in separate hotels and, of course, like the Jordanaires, earning a fraction of what he did with their more modest salaries; $200 dollars a week when they were working and $100 a week when they weren't. The whirling wind of fame was heartless and about to blow them away.

With no word from the military about the draft, Elvis went home to Graceland, where he now had five members of his immediate family working for him. It was a welcome respite, but it brought a problem to light that worried Elvis. It wasn't Gladys's complaints about the Colonel, those he was used to. Neither was it Anita Wood, a lovely blonde model, who soon had her own room at the house and who Gladys liked. The problem was Gladys herself.

His mother worried a lot; about the way Parker treated her son, about him flying, about him being killed in the military; and she was lonely in the big house and missed him being at home. Her health was deteriorating, too; she was putting on weight, her legs had become larger and her movements slower; there were dark, puffy rings beneath her eyes. And she was drinking vodka.

But the voracious music industry allowed no adjournments for personal problems, and Elvis went back to the studio to record what would become his biggest-selling long-playing release of all time; Elvis's Christmas Album – even though Irving Berlin had asked radio stations not to play the Elvis version of 'White Christmas'. Unfortunately, there was worse news than that in the pipeline.

Scotty and Bill had long been peeved that their salaries hadn't increased, and they suggested to Elvis that an instrumental album with him on piano might help to bring them in a few more dollars. Elvis agreed, but when Parker found out he had the project cancelled, to Elvis's great embarrassment. The boys had had enough. They immediately flew home, and in their wake a few days later came their resignation letter. Elvis called them, tried to sort out the mess, but it proved impossible to do. It was a very sad ending to a friendship that had helped to launch Elvis's career and supported him so well in the early days.

Elvis missed them.

Not long after, he rang Scotty to offer them $250 per show each for some concerts in California and Hawaii. They accepted. But there had been a fracture; the old times would never return.

Fame and fortune were already proving to be heartless companions. Even during that successful year of 1957, he mentioned on different occasions that he wasn't happy despite the success. Gladys was visibly unwell and often on the edge of tears. Nonetheless, she did her best to help her son, and he was glad to have her to unburden himself to. He worried, too, that his voice would suffer during his time in the military. He was soon to find out, because someone from the Memphis Draft Board arrived at Graceland just before Christmas. Parker insisted he be given no special status. Elvis would be just a regular GI. The army agreed to a deferment of a few months until March 1958. Before that, however, the moneymen needed to squeeze some more dollars from him; RCA wanted new records, Paramount wanted a new movie.

In August he celebrated his 23rd birthday and then set out for Hollywood and King Creole, based on the Harold Robbins book A Stone for Danny Fisher. And the familiar pattern was set up; the film's title was changed; it was given the name of a Jerry Leiber and Mike Stoller song. Yes, once again he would be singing. Then it would be Leiber and Stoller's turn to walk out on Elvis; and as before, Parker's intransigence was the catalyst, when he refused to allow Elvis to contemplate working on a project the songwriters had mooted to the star. They simply found him impossible to work with and they never combined talents with, or even saw, Elvis again.

Elvis finished his film with Walter Matthau and Dolores Hart, who was his love interest once more, met Sophia Loren, and later declared his character in the film, Danny Fisher, a 19-year-old, who becomes involved with two women and criminals, to have been his favourite role. Presley's acting ability was, at last, getting recognition, and a song from the film, 'Hard Headed Woman', went to number one on the Billboard pop singles chart. "*The star gives his best acting performance to date*", "*Presley shows signs that he is getting the hang of acting*" and "*The fellow isn't a bad actor*", the critics opined.

The fans loved him, so the film was a commercial as well as a critical success.

And then it was over. And so was life as Elvis Presley pop star knew it. The 5' 11" youngster, now sporting an army cropped haircut, looked as handsome as ever and was determined to be a hard-working, model soldier. The Colonel wanted it so.

The Colonel always got what he wanted from Elvis.

He w
mone
want
And
only
to ta
he w
A gr
perfo
Elvis
deliv
great
perfo
in a s
base
sensa
best-
"A St

Co-sta
CAROL
JON

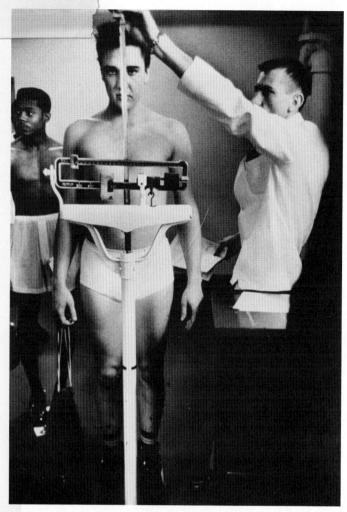

Elvis Presley clad in underwear as he stands on a set of scales while an Army doctor measures his height at a pre induction physical at Kennedy Veterans Hospital.

39

I DON'T HAVE A WOODEN HEART

Elvis knew that the world was waiting for the first signs of privileged behaviour on his part, or for the new recruit to fall flat on his face. He made the greatest efforts not to stand out and every effort to befriend his fellow recruits. During the basic ten-week training, he even lost weight, which made him look better than ever.

Now the centre of world attention, loneliness surrounded him more intensely than he had known it before. Nonetheless, celebrity status still brought him privileges not accorded to others; the sergeant allowed him to make phone calls from the sergeant's own home, where he was also allowed to meet up with Anita Wood. But when Elvis phoned home, he was miserable, even tearful; GI Presley had fallen into a depression, convinced that his career was over, that the world would forget him.

Those fears were not far-fetched, and RCA were well aware of them. For once, Elvis countered Parker's wishes, although the only concession he could squeeze from him was a one-night recording session at RCA's Nashville studios. Five recordings came out of that session including 'A Fool Such As I' and 'I Need Your Love Tonight'; six hours work and probably more than 5 million record sales would come from that night. Elvis was thrilled with the recordings, as was RCA.

Then it was back to base and Fort Hood, and as he had been assigned to the Third Armoured Division, its first task when he returned was tank training. GI Presley was off to West Germany.

It must have seemed to Elvis that the world was turning against him when Gladys contracted hepatitis and ended up in hospital. An urgent message prompted Elvis to apply for leave, and when it was granted, he flew immediately to the hospital in Memphis.

Leaving the hospital at midnight the following day with the promise to return, he was woken up at 3.30 in the morning by

Presley strolls the grounds of his Graceland estate in circa 1957

40

41

a phone call. Vernon didn't need to say a word; Elvis knew. Gladys was dead. Heart failure at 46 years of age.

It was a time for tears, and Elvis and Vernon could hardly breathe, so hard did they weep at Gladys' bedside. The singer's grief was so overwhelming that he went into a state of deep shock; it would stay with him for the rest of his life.

Son and mother had enjoyed a close relationship, perhaps too close, perhaps inhibiting Elvis's relationships with other women. *"I don't know why she had to go so young"*, he said later, but her demise made him think about death. Prophetically he added, *"I don't feel I'll live a long life. That's why I have to get what I can from every day"*.

Sleepless nights followed, **tranquilisers; then the awfulness of seeing his mother lying in her coffin.**

"Wake up mama. Wake up baby and talk to Elvis", he said to her, touching her hands and even hugging her. Those close to him began to worry if the heartbreak wasn't going to send him over the edge. The funeral director had to seal the coffin with a glass cover to keep him away from her. At the burial ceremony, he cried out and had to be restrained from stumbling towards the open grave.

"... everyone loves their mother, but I was an only child... it wasn't just like losing a mother, it was like losing a friend, a companion, someone to talk to. I could wake her up any hour of the night, and if I was worried or troubled about something she'd get up and try to help me". Elvis would never again find that unconditional closeness that he yearned for.

Elvis and father, Vernon discuss the illness of Elvis' mother outside her hospital room.

Graceland was teaming with people. From that point onwards, any semblance of normal life for Elvis took to its heels never to return. Colonel Parker had Elvis all to himself. The personal consequences for his protégé would be devastating.

As ever in Elvis's life, his personal emotions were given little time to be dealt with adequately. It was time to board the USS General George M. Randall for his new posting abroad. It would be a year and a half before he returned to the United States. A year and a half of conflicting emotions, when his intention to slot into life as an ordinary soldier was often challenged by the knowledge of what he had left behind. *"It ain't easy being one of the guys. I ain't never been one of the guys and I never will be one of the guys."*

Such sentiments never reached the public's ears.

42

There were consolation prizes; for a while, he was liberated from the demands of the music industry and the relentless push of the Colonel. And because he wasn't one of the guys, he was given permission to live off base during off duty hours in another large house he had rented in the nearby town of Bad Nauheim. There he installed his father, grandmother and his best friends Red West and Lamar Fike, well-known and liked for his sense of humour and outspoken honesty and a welcome rock in the shifting sands of Elvis's career. He would stay with Elvis until the singer's untimely death. Off base, therefore, he might just as well have been in America, with his boots polished for him – Lamar and Red working for spending money only – twelve handmade uniforms, a BMW for himself and a Cadillac for Vernon and life as normal, except without his mother, in the Presley bubble.

ACKNOWLEDGEMENT OF SERVICE OBLIGATION

I, _____Elvis Aron Presley_____, HAVING BEEN INDUCTED INTO THE ARMED SERVICES OF THE UNITED STATES ON THIS ___24th___ DAY OF __March__ 19_58_, FOR 2 YEARS ACTIVE DUTY, ACKNOWLEDGE THAT I HAVE B EEN INFORMED OF MY SERVICE OBLIGATION. I UNDERSTAND THAT UPON COMPLETION OF MY TERM OF ACTIVE DUTY I WILL, IF QUALIFIED, BE TRANSFERRED TO THE RESERVE AND REQUIRED TO SERVE THEREIN FOR A PERIOD WHICH, WHEN ADDED TO MY ACTIVE DUTY SERVICE, TOTALS 6 YEARS, UNLESS SOONER DISCHARGED IN ACCORDANCE WITH STANDARDS PRESCRIBED B Y THE SECRETARY OF DEFENSE: THAT I WILL BE REQUIRED TO SERVE A PERIOD IN THE READY RESERVE WHICH, WHEN ADDED TO MY ACTIVE DUTY SERVICE TOTALS 5 YEARS: THAT I MAY THEN, UPON WRITTEN REQUEST, BE TRANSFERRED TO THE STANDBY RESERVE FOR THE REMAINDER OF MY OBLIGATED PERIOD OF SERVICE. I FURTHER UNDERSTAND THAT DURING MY SERVICE AS A MEMBER OF THE READY RESERVE I WILL BE REQUIRED TO ATTEND NOT LESS THAN 48 SCHEDULE DRILLS OR TRAINING PERIODS AND NOT MORE THAN 17 DAYS ACTIVE DUTY FOR TRAININ ANNUALLY, OR THAT IN LIEU THEREOF, WHEN AUTHORIZED, I MAY BE REQUIRED TO PERFORM 30 DAYS ACTIVE DUTY FOR TRAINING ANNUALLY, THAT FAILURE TO PERFORM REQUIRED TRAINING IN ANY YEAR CAN RESULT IN MY BEING ORDERED TO PERFORM ADDITIONAL ACTIVE DUTY FOR TRAINING FOR 45 DAYS FOR THAT YEAR, AND IN HAVING MY SERVICE IN THE READY RESERVE EXTENDED INVOLUNTARILY.

Pvt E-1 Elvis Aron Presley
US- 53 310 761

MESSAGE

DEPARTMENT OF THE ARMY
STAFF COMMUNICATIONS OFFICE

PRECEDENCE	TYPE MSG (Check)		ACCOUNTING SYMBOL	ORIG. OR REFERS TO	CLASSIFICATION OF REFERENCE
ACTION ROUTINE	BOOK	MULTI	SINGLE	DA	
INFO			X		

FROM:

CINFO DA WASHDC

TO: CINCUSAREUR HEIDLEBERG GERMANY

SPECIAL INSTRUCTIONS

DIST:
TAG
DCSPER

DA343057   From CINFO for IO

1. The following statement has been released by
Fort Hood and is provided to you for guidance.

2. "Pvt. Elvis Presley completes Army basic indiv
tng May 31, at which time he becomes eligible for two
weeks' leave. On June 16 he will begin eight weeks of
advanced indiv tng as an Armor crewman. He subsequently
will complete his tng with the 2d Armored Division in a
six-week basic unit tng cycle, which ends Sep 20. At
that time Pvt. Presley will go to Germany as a packet
replacement for the 3d Armored Division of the Seventh
U.S. Army."

INFO

ASGNT BR

PERS REG BR

DATE 28	TIME 1045
MONTH May	YEAR 58

SYMBOL

CINFO-PI

WRITER

TYPED NAME AND TITLE (Signature, if required)
Maj Hooper, News/Feat Br.

PHONE 72351

PAGE NR. 1

NR. OF PAGES 1

SECURITY CLASSIFICATION

UNCLASSIFIED

SIGNATURE

Harold B. Yenderly

RELEASER

TYPED (or stamped) NAME AND TITLE

DANIEL PARKER
Colonel, GS
Chief, Public Information Division

ORIGIN: CI

DISTR : TAG, DCSPER

DA 343057   (MAY 58) DTG: 282009Z   nm/6

PAGE NR.

Of course, there were girls; fidelity was something for others – and especially expected in his girlfriends, and in Anita in particular – but not for the boy who was not like other guys. That boy was soon enjoying life with a German girl called Elizabeth Stefaniak, who was now a live-in and bed-in companion hired to take care of all the German fan mail. Sleeping beside her, however, was not the same as sleeping with her. And if she did not want to be subjected to his volcanic rages and a summary dismissal, she would do well not to see any other boys and not get too friendly with Red and Lamar; though she often had to endure other girls taking her place on Elvis's pillow. Selfishness was the other side of his generosity and both were lavished equally casually.

Elvis would always be happy when one of his team brought teenage girls to his house: that was how he met a young, confident American girl, still in ninth grade, called Priscilla Beaulieu. He fell for her the moment she walked through the door. Very quickly afterwards, he was playing the piano and singing for her before then leading her up to his bedroom. She would be a permanent feature of his life in Germany for the next seven months.

One sour note that introduced itself was when Vernon began an affair with Dee Stanley, the wife of an American serviceman, four months after the death of Gladys. Matters became heated, and for a while Vernon felt the sting of Elvis's self-righteous indignation, being sent back to Graceland in disgrace. To no avail, because Dee became his stepmother in 1960, although Elvis couldn't then, or ever, bring himself to like her.

Another friend in the military desert was Charlie Hodge, who sang with the Foggy River Boys and who Elvis knew about. Charlie had also studied singing; so Elvis's voice, instead of suffering from a prolonged period of inactivity as he had feared, was trained and developed by

43

Charlie. Trying out all kinds of new songs with Charlie's encouragement, he would already be in the starting blocks when he returned to the USA. Out of this training would evolve one of his biggest hits; 'It's Now or Never', his reworking of the Enrico Caruso version of 'O Solo Mio'.

And then the grumbling, the discontent, the German girls, the handmade uniforms along with army life faded into part of his romantic biography. On March the 3rd 1960, Sergeant Elvis Presley with three stripes on his arm, touched down at McGuire Air Force Base in New Jersey in the midst of a snowstorm.

Not quite everything from Germany faded away; Elizabeth Stefaniak went to Graceland as his secretary – only to take off a few months later with Rex Mansfield, a friend of Elvis's from the army – and Priscilla would soon be there, too. As would Anita and many others.

"The army teaches boys to think like men", he would say later. But his idea of manhood had, perhaps, been somewhat skewed, was not quite what other guys thought it was. No longer the sweet youth that had left America, distraught at having lost his mother, there was now a slightly unpleasant...

...air of arrogance about Elvis Presley on 'civvie street'.

44

---

8 September 1959

Honorable Frank Kowalski

House of Representatives

Dear Mr. Kowalski:

This letter is in reply to your inquiry concerning an early release from active duty of Specialist Four Elvis Presley on the basis of good behavior.

You may be assured that there is no provision for early release of Army personnel on the basis of good behavior. The normal expiration of Specialist Presley's term of service is 23 March 1960. In accordance with established rotation policies, he is scheduled to depart the oversea command on or about 3 March 1960 for return to the United States for release from active duty.

The Army endeavors to be completely impartial to all its personnel. Accordingly, the Army tries neither to discriminate against individuals on the basis of their status as public figures nor to grant them special privileges.

Your interest in this matter is appreciated.

Sincerely,

VERNE L. BOWERS
Lt Colonel, GS
Office, Chief of
Legislative Liaison

cc: TAG

MHQ/73231/ime

M/R: Reply based on ltr to Rep Monagan, 26 Aug 59.
ime

OUT
8 SEP 1959
Office Chief of
Legislative
Liaison

45

Presley poses for a portrait in circa 1960

"YOUR CHEATIN' HEART"

The Frank Sinatra Timex show had offered Elvis $125,000 for just two songs, a phenomenal amount of money; it hadn't taken long for the Colonel to rope his protégé back onto the wagon again. By then, he'd already spent time in the studio recording the first of a dozen 'new' songs that RCA were apoplectic to get their hands on. Nor had it taken long for the wily Sinatra to see which way the wind was blowing in the music scene, reverse the biting sarcasm of his opinions and try to bathe in the young star's reflected glory; with a duet of 'Love Me Tender', for example.

When asked about the Sinatra-Presley relationship, D. J. Fontana commented, *"I think they did a good job together. I think Sinatra kind of got on his side after a while, he wasn't sure about how they would like each other... they were laughing and grinning and having a good time in rehearsals, and they all seemed like they really got along fine".*

Out of the resumed sessions in the studio in Nashville came evergreen songs such as 'Are You Lonesome Tonight', 'It's Now or Never' and 'Such a Night'. Thanks to the time in Germany spent with Charlie, Elvis's voice had more depth, fullness and elasticity; his vocal range had increased, his control had become more assured. He was ready to reconquer the heights. Everyone was pleasantly surprised.

With the Colonel now unchallenged at the head of Elvis's career, he soon had Elvis filming a new movie; it didn't matter that his star was disappointed in a vehicle intended, once again, to exploit his singing rather than his acting talent. Inevitably, perhaps, the film was called GI Blues; good-looking guy meets good-looking gals for fun and games in the army in Germany and croons a series of uninspiring songs at them.

Elvis and his manager were definitely not playing from the same song sheet, on which were printed, almost exclusively, songs by Julian and Jean Aberbach, with whom Elvis had naïvely been persuaded to sign a publishing deal. Now the Colonel would only allow their songs to be sung so the royalties would stay 'in house'. As Elvis knew to his detriment, their songs were not in his league. It was hard to argue against box office receipts, however, and the film reaching the number two spot in the Variety national box office chart did help to fund those parties chock-a-block with girls and amphetamines – as indeed, did 'It's Now or Never', which had gone off to conquer the world and break records in what would become a nine-million unit selling spree. And besides, filming was all over within a few weeks as usual.

Only in one respect did Elvis's personal life change greatly that year of 1960; Vernon married Dee in July, and although Elvis hated the fact that she would usurp his mother's position at Graceland, he was happy to see Dee's three young sons at the house.

The gap Gladys' death had torn into Elvis's life was palpable. She had been his moral yardstick; ignored, it's true, but he seemed to have needed her moral standpoint as

46

a shield against criticism by others of his own behaviour – he was then able to excuse it in his own head. *"If I never do anything really wrong"*, he once said, *"it's all because of her"*.

Another film, Flaming Star, soon took up more of his time – and more of his aggravation. Again the songs were the fly in the ointment. Neither fans nor critics were particularly impressed with the film, even though they decided that Presley's role, Pacer Burton, born of a Kiowa mother and a Texan father on the Texan frontier, produced his best acting performance to date, as the boy struggling

47

Frank Sinatra welcomes back Rock and Roll star Elvis Presley after his stint in the US army on his self titled TV variety show on March 26, 1960

Valentines card from 1960

to reconcile cultural conflicts. For his part, Elvis already felt disillusionment with Hollywood setting in. Parker, though, saw on which side his bread was buttered and light musical fair was what the fans would get from Presley as long as he had anything to do with it.

And he did, of course, thrusting a third movie upon Elvis that year. Released just one month after GI Blues, Wild in the Country was yet another Presley film in which he had a straight acting role that missed its mark with fans and critics. The singer's mood was not the best; he knew this kind of insipid film was not going to give him the breakthrough in film that he desired.

Scotty's view was clear; "*I just wish he could have got some real scripts later on. When they found out they could make some money off of him, I guess, well, he went ahead and did it – I never will understand why. He just wouldn't put his foot down on management and say, "I will not do this. Give me something."* He did have a chance at A Star is Born – they *had that in mind for him, and then Parker wouldn't let him do it*".

Not that Elvis concentrated upon Wild in the Country any more than he did on any other film, always ready as he was for the distraction of girls and his entourage around the set. Success – and his success was now truly phenomenal, his records having uncorked a waterfall of dollars for everyone involved – had gripped him tightly in a tango towards destruction. Shielded from the world by what the press now termed the "*Memphis Mafia*", a gaggle of favoured friends and relatives, none of whom earned much more than their expenses once they were in the favourite's circle, his entourage ensured that the boss was kept happy with jokes and instant approval of everything he said so that reality, and those doubting voices in his head, those little serpents of disapproval, were kept at bay. Rules

Poster for G.I. Blues

Various images from the film

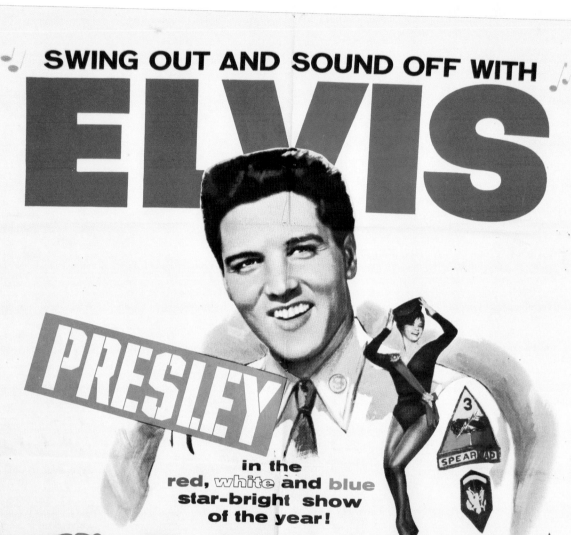

SWING OUT AND SOUND OFF WITH

ELVIS
PRESLEY

in the
red, white and blue
star-bright show
of the year!

♪♫ G·I·BLUES ♫♪

A **HAL WALLIS** PRODUCTION

☆☆☆☆☆☆☆☆☆☆☆☆☆
TECHNICOLOR®
☆☆☆☆☆☆☆☆☆☆☆☆☆

ELVIS SCORES...

A SINGING TRIUMPH...

AND A ROMANTIC HIT!

Co-starring
JULIET PROWSE   Directed by NORMAN TAUROG · Written by EDMUND BELOIN
and HENRY GARSON · A PARAMOUNT RELEASE

COPYRIGHT © 1960 BY HAL B. WALLIS & JOSEPH H. HAZEN   60-1935

German poster for Blue Hawaii

Presley poses for the release of his film `It Happened At The World's Fair` in September 1962 at MGM Studios, California

50

he lay down for the entourage at Graceland and elsewhere were the law, they were challenged at your own peril. Elvis was 25-years old and lord of almost everything and all of those he surveyed; that's how he liked it; being powerful was an aphrodisiac. True, the Colonel might be the puppet master, but the puppet had his own marionettes to shout at and bully.

Scotty's opinion contained more sadness than criticism of his former front man; "*Well, he was just a regular guy. With all the stuff that hit him at such an early age and so fast – he never really had a chance to grow up. He always had his so-called friends around him and he just never grew up*".

Perhaps he wasn't growing up, but at just 26 years of age he was certainly already growing outwards. Hal Wallis told him so, too, when he turned up for work in Hawaii for his next romp through another song and sexy girls movie, Blue Hawaii. It mattered not to Elvis that it would become his film with the biggest box office ever and spawn a best-selling album; he was unhappy. Again the songs and the storyline were not to his liking. This was not the route he had wanted his movie career to take. Fans were happy to see him in this light fare, it seemed, and 'Can't Help Falling in Love' became one of his most loved hits. But where had the rebellious teenager gone? Where the rock and roll king? As a new generation of kids found new heroes, Parker had successfully turned Elvis into a soothingly anodyne symbol of wholesome youth, rebelling so gently that he wouldn't frighten anyone's maiden aunt or, more importantly, damage the money tree. Elvis didn't want to damage it, either, he had Graceland, its staff and a home in Bel Air to maintain; $500,000 a movie plus 25% of net profits was hard, impossible, to refuse. He felt, too, that he was indebted to Parker for his career, so he said nothing, memorised his words and worked hard at "*the job*".

"*I sure lost my musical direction in Hollywood*", he lamented. "*My songs were the same conveyer belt mass production, just like most of my movies were... those movies sure got me into a rut*".

Those films were becoming more important than the songs, too, in terms of income. One film loomed up every few months now, and it would have broken the singer's heart had he known that for the next five years, until 1967, fifteen films would feature him in formulaic pretty gals and handsome guy singing plots, entertainment that Parker had determined would rake in the dollars. Whether the songs were idiotic or not was of no concern when he was taking 25% commission from his star and percentages from

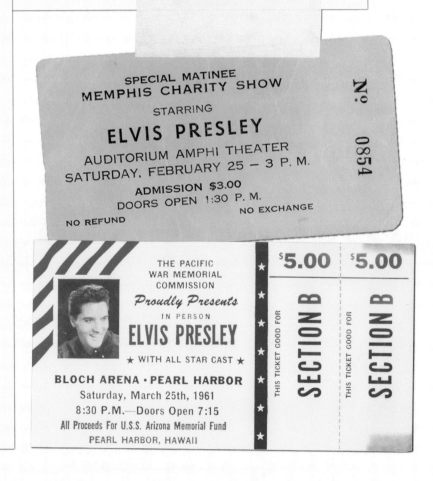

Concert tickets from 61

the publishing companies. Not one script did he bother to read. The Greenback count told him all he wanted to know. So the songs had to be written by 'in house' writers to keep the royalties rolling into Hill and Range, the Aberbachs' publishing companies. Such conveyor-belt songwriting could produce quantity but not quality. Elvis knew it, hated it, sang on to keep everyone happy.
"There are too many people that depend on me. I'm too obligated. I'm in too far to get out", was Elvis's sad comment upon his predicament.

Life as a wealthy man in a bubble of his own making contained parties, girls, of course – and for all-round enjoyment of them, he had installed a two-way mirror in the pool changing room – visits to Las Vegas and time spent with the guys at Bel Air. Those girls might have spent a night or longer with Elvis, but he was still attracted to one girl more than the others, a girl to whom

he felt he could unburden himself, who listened, as Gladys had done. So there were telephone calls to Priscilla, still at school in Germany. To her parents he suggested she come over to see him in Los Angeles. Graceland seemed less enticing without Gladys and with Dee slowly taking over.

Dee would soon feel his displeasure when Elvis finally forced Vernon and her to move out. This wasn't the only way that life somehow didn't seem to be what it had been shaping up to become. So Priscilla was a lifeline, a confidante, and he needed that badly, because he always had to be on show for the guys; with Priscilla he could relax his guard. And on top of that, her youthful naivety attracted him.

Until she came, there was another trip to Hawaii to distract him and a film with Elvis breaking into song as a charter boat captain. No doubt this time about the movie's content; it was called Girls, Girls, Girls. Still, an impoverished, singing Hawaiian fisherman brought the film a Golden Globe nomination in its wake.

Parker was hard at work, because the next girl-buster film, It Happened at the World's Fair, in which he played a debt ridden crop-dusting pilot, wasn't far behind. Yes, of course, he was singing; but the fans were singularly unimpressed, even though he was in better form than he had been and the songs were not as bad as he had feared they would be.

Elvis was back in California in time for 17-year-old Priscilla's arrival in June of 1962. She was immediately whisked to the singer's house in Bel-Air for a two-week stay during which time she only spent one night away from the singer's bed, whatever he might have said to her parents to persuade them such a thing would never happen. Neither would he have mentioned the amphetamines and sleeping pills that everyone,

Presley and actresses promoting Girls Girls Girls

Poster for Girls Girls Girls

54

Priscilla with her dog, Honey, at Memphis International airport, Memphis, Tennessee, 11th January 1963

including Priscilla, swallowed like sweets to make life go with a swing.

For Priscilla, life became a kaleidoscopic fairground ride, peopled with Elvis's sycophantic entourage, and driven by the magnetic power of fame, and it culminated in an explosion of lavishness when he took her for two weeks in Las Vegas, where he spent thousands of dollars to have his youthful conquest draped with the glamorous accoutrements he loved, transforming the fresh-faced schoolgirl into a false-eyelash and mascara wielding, gaudily dressed doll, his perfect female.

And she soon discovered that the perfect female has nothing substantial to say to the perfect male, when Elvis turned from charmer to demon and back after she had innocently proclaimed that she preferred his rock 'n' roll to some of his other music. She learned a valuable lesson for her future life with him; never criticise a gift horse to his face.

Soon after Priscilla's departure for Germany again, however, it was Anita who committed the ultimate crime in Elvis's eyes; she left him – when she overheard him discussing Priscilla.

So then there was one; and Elvis completed his coup d'etat when – after many soothingly hypocritical phone calls to Priscilla's parents in Germany – father Beaulieu brought Priscilla over to the US himself so that she could live in Graceland where, her father thought, she would be watched over by Vernon and Dee in a house adjacent to the main house and attend school in California. Within a whisker of time she was back in Elvis's bed in Graceland and living in Graceland itself, which concerned everyone as she was still underage. No one said a word. Not even the local press, who must have had their suspicions about the local boy's behaviour. Not Parker, not one friend. Elvis's career, and therefore their lives, their financial welfare, depended on silence. It was March 1963. The rollercoaster ride was underway.

Priscilla, too, was damned to a life in secret; the price for her privileged position was no schoolgirl life, no school friends in the house let alone the bedroom for homework together. It was lonely, and Elvis denied her existence whilst denying to her that he was having affairs with his Hollywood ladies. Which he was. Yet he refused to have sex with her, although she was willing, despite being passionate but not "*overtly sexual*" towards his girlfriend. In Priscilla's version of the state of play in the bedroom, Elvis had said, "*I'm not saying we can't do other things. It's just the actual encounter. I want to save it*". Photographs of her dressed in her school uniform in sexy poses were more to his taste, it seemed.

Neither could she befriend anyone in the house; his eagle-eyed jealousy taught her to be wary of speaking to the men in his entourage. Was she nothing more than a live-in plaything in a gilded cage? Nothing more than a live comforter, a favourite blanket of his very own?

Had she known what was happening off the set of Viva Las Vegas, the next film he'd been engaged to sing in, Priscilla might have realised which way the wind blew.

Viva Las Vegas wasn't a bad Elvis movie at all, despite many critics being lukewarm about it and it garnered some "*Unimportant as a banana split*" reviews. In fact, Elvis was in third place for the 1965 Laurel Award for best male performance in a musical film and fans liked what Elvis was delivering, enough to make it one of his most popular films, this time as Lucky Jackson who ends up with the love interest of Ann-Margret.

On and off the screen, the chemistry crackled between the two, and the entourage was treated to the sight of Elvis and Ann-Margret riding off on two motorcycles for their trysts. For the Colonel, this was a step too far, because the film had overrun its budget. It was an Elvis film not a co-operative effort, and he made sure that the film's duets between the lovers were left on the cutting room floor, and her close ups likewise. Any effective protests on Elvis's part, as usual, failed to materialize, even though Ann-Margret had turned his head and made him seriously doubt the sagacity of his relationship with Priscilla. Phone calls to his new flame every day followed the end of shooting.

But Ann-Margret was not the woman Elvis wanted, although it took him until Christmas of 1963 to realise it. Ann-Margret was an independent woman. Elvis was not an independent man, but he wanted a dependent woman who would look after him like his mom used to. Perhaps unaware of the role assigned to her, Priscilla was shaping up to be that woman.

Elvis and Ann-Margret had run their course as lovers. Friendship would remain.

Priscilla was safe for another day.

"UNEASY LIES THE HEAD THAT WEARS A CROWN"

Presley picture is the only sure thing in Hollywood", said Hal Wallis, who produced nine of the 27 pictures that Elvis would make in the 1960s, most of them critically panned, all of them helping to make Elvis – and the Colonel, which was the main point of them, it seems – wealthy; three times wealthier than his songs did, in fact, in every year of that decade. In 1964, he earned $506,000 from his music. The films, on the other hand brought in $1,508,000. Sometimes he would shoot three features in one year.

Elvis needed the money because he spent prolifically. On top of paying taxes that might amount to over $700,000 in a year in which he earned $2,000,000. And spending helped to keep the black dog of depression at bay.

Depression? Elvis must have known that he was Parker's poodle, that Parker had one hold over him that could never be removed, a hold that made Elvis submit like a child to the Colonel's wishes, when he behaved like a Pasha to everyone else. Fear. Fear of poverty. That fear marbled both his and Vernon's every waking hour. And secondly, the fear of losing fame, of not being recognised, of not bathing in the adoration of the fans who gathered outside the gates of Graceland.

Four dire movies, "*bargain basement templates*", as writer Ray Connolly described them, would follow Viva Las Vegas! into 1964. Elvis's singing career seemed to have gone to bed loaded with sleeping pills; was there any sign of life in it at all? All that he was known for now were those insipid movie soundtracks, and they began to sell less and less well

as Elvis's name and fame as a rebellious and powerful singer turned from gold to silver and then to bronze.

It was a dangerous time for a singer to remain dormant. Elvis had noticed that, whilst he'd been tied down in Hollywood, the music scene had changed dramatically. There were insurgents all around. In fact, he was being usurped in no uncertain style, especially by four Mop Tops from the other side of the Atlantic. Four lads from Liverpool were conquering America with quips, smart retorts, grinning cheekiness and their sheer joie de vivre, not to mention their inventive, infectious song rhythms. Jealously, he remembered that this had been him not so long ago, the butt of Sinatra and Dino's ire, before he had forced them to the ground and submission with a swing of the hips and a whirl of his arm.

Elvis watched the Fab Four on TV, saw that they had 5 top ten singles in the US and knew that he should be worried. But Hollywood sucked him back in, another soapy script that was hardly worth reading. It brought him the money, but Elvis and Priscilla both disliked Hollywood and most of the people they met there. The Colonel's remark that a Presley movie was only good for making money certainly didn't help his attitude towards Hollywood or towards his manager, who, he gradually realised, might be singing from a different song sheet than he was.

As movies and rare sessions of singing took up, at most, four months of his life, he spent the rest of the time watching others in movies he liked; Peter Sellers in Dr. Strangelove, Tom Jones, It's a Wonderful Life, The Robe, and a film by

those four usurpers the Beatles, A Hard Day's Night. And being Elvis Presley, he was able to rent his local movie theatre for himself, where he would sit through the night. Released out into the world, he would go home to Bel Air to watch TV series and football games or join in the never-ending parties or read. He did a lot of reading.

There was another distraction that year that Elvis indulged in, which served to aggravate most of those around him. Elvis read the Bible throughout his life and never understood, or chose to ignore, the contradictions, the impossibility of reconciling its teachings with his own desires – maybe that friction caused some of those tantrums that littered his personal life. He would read from the Bible to his entourage and Priscilla, usually only reaping amusement, to his annoyance. But for him, it was all real, and he had become uncertain of what God had intended his life to achieve in a spiritual sense. That voice of his was a gift from Him, after all, so what purpose did he want Elvis to serve with it?

By coincidence, he found himself in the grip of a spiritual growth journey, when the hairdresser who arrived at his house one day was not his favoured coiffeur but a man

Poster for Viva Las Vegas

Above left   Elvis Presley recording a movie soundtrack in a recording studio in circa 1964 in Los Angeles, California

58

Elvis Presley in movie stills from circa 1964

525,720
Already shipped
ELVIS'
new single
#8740

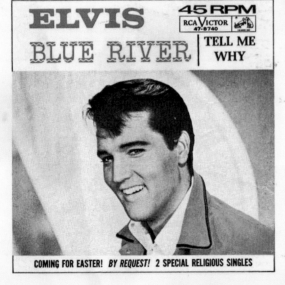

ELVIS	45 RPM
BLUE RIVER	RCA VICTOR 47-8740
	TELL ME WHY

COMING FOR EASTER! *BY REQUEST!* 2 SPECIAL RELIGIOUS SINGLES

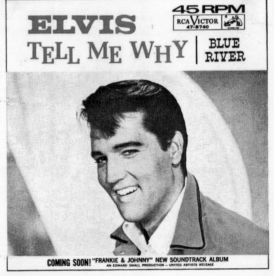

ELVIS	45 RPM
TELL ME WHY	RCA VICTOR 47-8740
	BLUE RIVER

COMING SOON! "FRANKIE & JOHNNY" NEW SOUNDTRACK ALBUM
AN EDWARD SMALL PRODUCTION — UNITED ARTISTS RELEASE

RCA Victor
RCA The most trusted name in sound

A billboard classic '45 ad

named Larry Geller. Geller was deeply interested in the New Age religions and spiritual searches that were splashing about in the sixties, and Elvis, who had never been greatly interested in books, soon found himself devouring The Autobiography of a Yogi, amongst other tomes. Elvis was a man obsessed. The entourage were envious of the bond that had developed; Priscilla liked Geller but was aggrieved that his theories gave Elvis another set of reasons not to have sex with her, and the Colonel was ready to burst that his client was now sounding unbalanced and talking about forming communes and emotional balance. Parker would have to fume about it for a further two years, whilst Elvis had visions; until, in fact, he was dissuaded from abandoning his career by another guru.

Priscilla? Well, she was up to Elvis's tricks. She had come thus far and she would not fall at the line. As Elvis bowed to Parker's wishes, so Priscilla learned to bow to Elvis's; not for her the further education of her former classmates; the King did not want an educated female to call him out. Instead, he wanted glamour, he wanted feminine grace and feminine subordination. She knew that Elvis was using her as a living doll and as a projection of his ideal woman with short, short skirts, dyed black hair, heavy make-up and dark, dark eyeliner. She went along with the game. Rumours were doing the rounds; that Priscilla had threatened to inform the press about her relationship should Elvis refuse to marry her. There was also a story that without marriage, father Beaulieu would see Elvis charged under the Mann Act for taking a minor across state lines for sexual purposes. There was only one exit from that road and Parker would steer Elvis to it and out under the sign.

1964 moved over for 1965, and it seemed as though life would trundle along as it had done for years now. The stream of tepid movies did not abate and four more went out into the world that year with Paradise, Hawaiian Style marking Elvis's third visit to the Pacific island. The movie soundtracks constituted the bulk of his singing output, and their quality diminished along with the quality of the film scripts.

RCA was desperate for something from Elvis to be put onto the music market before he vanished completely beneath the tidal wave of Beatles and Rolling Stones and, in what turned out to be a golden idea, decided to put out a single; 'Crying in the Chapel'. Confounding everyone's expectations, it hit number one in United Kingdom and even got to number three in the US, his only top 10 hit between 1964 and 1968.

That British tidal wave flooded into his front room one day when the Beatles paid him a visit. It was about as starchy as a clergyman's collar, with Elvis being cagey and the women, Priscilla included, silent. The Fab Four quipped in their usual manner, which, together with their long hair, and the knowledge of their success, only served to make Elvis feel outdated and out of the loop. As they left, there was no intention on his part about accepting an invitation to visit the Beatles at home. And when he heard about the death of his former bandmate, bassist Bill Black, he must have wondered if his own era was also drawing to some kind of close.

The success of 'Crying in the Chapel' had galvanised Elvis himself. They decided that it was time for another album, and in view of that success and the fact that Elvis was thought of as perhaps the greatest white gospel singer of the age, Elvis returned to the music studio in May 1966 to record a gospel/religious album. Elvis wanted this music to be expansive, to incorporate a church choir, to have a big, full sound. He was excited at this new project, happy to be singing music he loved. RCA, of course, wanted some hit singles, a difficult thing to achieve, as Elvis had been disengaged from his past and his fans for so long with his sugar-candy movies and soundtracks. Religious songs were hardly going to compete with the likes of Bob Dylan, The Rolling Stones and The Troggs. RCA were to remain disappointed on that score, although the album itself, How

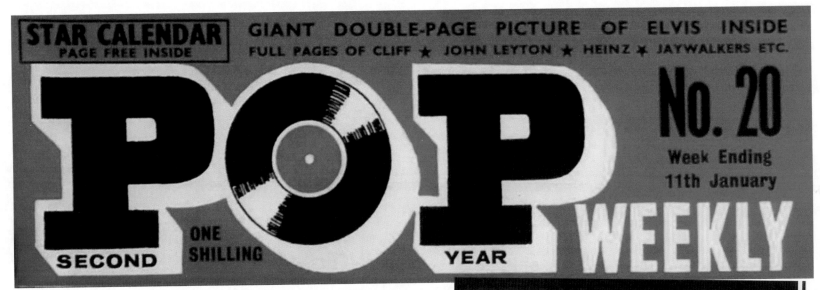

60

Great Thou Art, would eventually be awarded a Grammy as the best sacred album of 1967, earning many positive reviews.

Any elation that Elvis might have felt in a recording studio enjoyed a short shelf life. Elvis was falling prey to depressions again; hardly surprising considering his intake of prescription drugs, those little helpers that the Colonel had once given him to keep him going at night and get him up in the morning; barbiturates, painkillers and sleeping pills that taken together produced a delicious, soporific euphoria. They were necessary, too, to keep him on the conveyor belt of movies that never stopped. Easy Come, Easy Go, came in early 1967, a film in which he played a deep sea diving nightclub singer; you can't sing under water after all. Although Elvis might well have thought that singing underwater would have made no difference to the song 'Yoga Is As Yoga Does'.

His relentless schedule was evident as his 24th film, Double Trouble, came just thirteen days after Easy Come Easy Go was released on March the 22nd.

Those drugs probably came in handy to blot out the knowledge that the King had become a joke, not only in Hollywood, but in the music industry, too. RCA were beginning to recognise that they were sucking the life from their Elvis franchise; the language they finally understood was falling revenues.

Producer Hal Wallis had called it a day on Elvis films, too, no longer able to tolerate Parker's constant demands. And Parker was more emboldened than ever and wanting to tie Elvis into an even worse contract from which the Colonel would bump up his some of his take in the Elvis money tree to 50%. Their relationship had now morphed into a partnership. Elvis did not demur. Whichever way he looked, Elvis could see nothing but a slippery slope downwards. Both his film and singing careers were drying up. And to top it all, there was the thorny question of Priscilla. Parker would have been very well aware of the morality clauses in the singer's contracts, and the huge problems that any revelations about his domestic life might bring down on Elvis's head. Conflicting rumours circulated about his willingness to walk down the isle. According to some, he was "*crying at the thought*" and left with "*no choice*" but to marry.

Towards the end of 1966, he had caved in under the pressure and proposed to her at last, whether he had wanted to or not. Depressions plagued him. So did his weight. He did not want to film his 20th movie now that he was "*fat as pig*" as he described himself; shooting had to be postponed because of his size. Before the shoot, Elvis slipped and concussed himself, very probably full of prescription drugs.

When it finally got through to being released, Clambake, the "*silly, tired little frolic*", as the New York Times critic called it, saw its soundtrack record achieve the lowest sales ever for an Elvis soundtrack, though the movie reached number 15 on the national weekly box-office charts.

Elvis needed the money. He'd bought a ranch behind Graceland – he called it Circle G Ranch – which cost him $450,000, and he splashed out a fortune on horses, pickup trucks and riding gear for his entourage. The obsession lasted for only about one and a half years. Then, to Vernon's delight, Elvis had either tired of the ranch or the expense of running it and sold it for $440,000, together with everything else he had bought to feed the obsession.

Parker, sensing his star and money fountain dangerously close to a collapsed career, read the riot act to a humbled Elvis in front of the gathered household, warning him that Graceland would be lost if he carried on as he had been doing. Parker wanted change, wanted Elvis chaperoned, wanted some of the staff gone. He had his way as usual with not a word of opposition from Elvis, and re-established his powerful position. Geller was one of those chopped out of the

loop, and though Elvis burned some of the spiritual books, to Priscilla's delight as she thought that they had been a cause of confusion for the singer, he kept his favourite for the rest of his life; The Prophet by Kahlil Gibran.

Elvis's best friend, Red, was soon to be sidelined, too, uninvited to the singer's wedding. Hurt by Elvis's lack of loyalty,

Red decided to never again work for him.

Promoting the movie Clambake, directed by Arthur H. Nadel

"ALL ROADS LEAD TO VEGAS"

Priscilla maintained that she was a virgin when she and Elvis married in a suite at the Aladdin Hotel in Las Vegas on May the 1st 1967. At last, Vernon, Parker and father Beaulieu were satisfied. Elvis was thirty-two years old, and the original sexual thrill that had attached to the youthful Priscilla had been transformed into a more mundane love after so many years. Probably she felt the same. How would it all work out? Would he feel trapped? The adoring girls weren't going to vanish overnight or let marriage stop them; nor would he; he enjoyed that part of stardom too much.

One hundred guests turned up for the wedding breakfast, and the couple then flew off to Palm Springs, where Elvis had now found another house to help him escape the claustrophobic atmosphere of Hollywood. Then it was back to the Circle G for horse riding, picnics and a brief period, when Elvis and Priscilla almost lived a normal life as a couple. It would soon fly away never to return.

But Priscilla now had another grip on Elvis's life. She was pregnant.

Another mouth to feed, another film to help feed it. Elvis was back in Hollywood for Stay Away Joe and then Speedway. The latter film was notable for achieving the lowest sales of all Presley's soundtrack albums, and helped pull the plug on the format and his film musical career. Hardly surprising when The Beatles and Sgt Pepper, The Doors, Velvet Underground and Jefferson Airplane were the hot

tickets in town. But he was paired with Nancy Sinatra as his IRS agent love interest, and having lost weight, he notched up one of his best performances, as racing driver with a heart of gold Steve Grayson.

Any respect for Elvis's singing career had long since evaporated. Regarded as a has-been, if he were to climb back onto the wagon and have a chance of competing, he needed something strong. Between January 1967 and May 1968, he had recorded eight singles and only two had even made the top 40. Now his eye lighted on 'Guitar Man' by Jerry Reed, and delighted, Elvis enjoyed recording with the man himself to produce a minor hit in the country and pop world, where the single reached number 1 for one week on the country chart and number 43 on the Billboard Hot 100. Well, he still hadn't set the world on fire, but at least he was recording the kind of songs he liked again.

Elvis had a third film, Live a Little, Love a Little, slated for 1968, for which he recorded the soundtrack in March before his marriage. Another version of one of the songs, A Little Less Conversation, became a remix in 2002 and saw Elvis return to the international music sales charts. The movie made such a bad impression that it was never released in the UK.

Parker in the meantime, like RCA, having wrung almost all the money he could ($1,000,000 per film) from Elvis's movie career – although Elvis would be on set for three more in 1969 – realised very late that the wind had changed; he needed to go on a new tack rapidly if his client was not to be submerged by obscurity. There was only one way to tack that offered any chance of success; television. It was a fortunate choice. For Elvis, the man whose recording and movie careers were becoming extinct, the winds of change were about to bring his ship back into port laden down with treasures.

In 1968, Priscilla brought another little treasure of her own into the world for the singer. Her name was Lisa Marie, born on the 1st of February.

There was more good news, too: for one of the only occasions in his life when he would act independently of Parker, who had pitched the idea of an Elvis Christmas special to NBC TV, Elvis told TV executives that this was a chance for him to showcase all of his talents and not do yet more insipid songs. The executives could not resist the bait. What became known as the 'Comeback Special', was recorded in late June in Burbank, California with director Steve Binder, who had a talent for filming music concerts.

Elvis was "*scared to death*" about appearing in front of a live audience for the first time in seven years, since Hawaii 1961, and fell prey to a panic attack, fearing that the audience would mock him. Never before had he been asked for his input into the creation of a show, and he included all of his favourite genres from gospel to rock 'n' roll, ballads and blues. Scotty – he would play with Elvis for the last time during these sessions – and D. J. Fontana were brought into ease the singer's nerves, and the whole live segment became an improvised session that, with Elvis clad in tight black leather romping through some of his favourite songs, became the hit segment of the show.

And one song, 'If I Can Dream', written at Binder's behest to put the audience in tune with Elvis's reactions to the murders of J. F. Kennedy and Martin Luther King, would later reach number twelve in the US charts. Parker had not wanted to record the song, but Elvis overruled him with

63

The Wedding of Elvis Presley to Priscilla on May 01, 1967

64

a Western, the only Presley film in which he did not sing and there were no other songs apart from the title theme. Elvis also sported a beard. It was not a success, the least watched of all Elvis's films.

Next into the corral was the Trouble with Girls, in which Elvis played the manager of a travelling troupe. Singing again. There was less money up front this time, $850,000, and the film wasn't a success, either, though opinions changed after his death.

The era of Elvis movies was drawing to a close; there would only be one more.

December 1968 finally came around, and on the third,

the words "*We're doing it*".

It was all proof that Elvis had finally understood that he was the important person in the room not Parker. And, as so often, his instincts proved correct. He, and not Parker, had rescued his career at the last minute. It was a tragedy that he did not make greater use of his newfound power.

When Elvis listened to the tape of the show he was elated, and he turned to Binder and said, "*Steve, it's the greatest thing I've ever done in my life*".

In the interval between editing and release of the TV show, although Elvis, buoyed by his success in the studio, was keen to return to live stage performances, Parker had slotted in two more films after the NBC sessions. One of them gave Elvis a chance at a straight role; Charro! was

Elvis Presley performing on the Elvis comeback TV special on June 27, 1968

Priscilla and thirty-three-year-old Elvis settled in to watch the screening of his special on NBC. Binder had engaged scriptwriters to sculpt a show that contained specific themes with extravagant gospel-style musical sequences and a mini movie that was semi-autobiographical for Elvis, which had the song 'Guitar Man' as its fulcrum. Presley's hits were given the big production number treatment with lavish set designs. Elvis watched and saw where his future lay. Many critics missed the correct interpretation of what they were seeing, although others understood and also praised his staying power.

The show brought in the biggest ratings of the year for NBC; 42% of America had watched Elvis rising up from the dead.

Musically revived, Elvis arranged to go back into the studio for a follow-up album in January 1969. The place chosen was the American Sound Studio in Memphis, where the soul sound of the house band, 'The Memphis Boys', proved to be an inspired choice, as did producer Chips Moman. He emphasised the rhythm section and brought in electric blues, country, rural and gospel elements.

Elvis was happy and recording sessions went well. The songs included, 'Gentle on My Mind', 'I'll Hold You in My Heart', 'Long Black Limousine', and a song that would catapult Elvis back into public awareness; 'In the Ghetto'. Although there was a worry that a white guy singing about ghetto life would not go down well, Elvis was not perturbed, and it became one of his greatest hits. On a high, engaged in a uniquely productive recording experience, Elvis wanted to get hold of all the good songs that he could lay his hands on and told everyone so, even if it meant going outside his and Parker's own publishing house. The priority was to make good records, and from

now on, as Elvis said in no uncertain terms, if you wanted to do a song, he was going to do it.

When Parker got wind of another Presley insurrection, his scathingly vicious comment was, "*let him fall on his ass*". It would not be Elvis but Parker, who that fate would eventually take down.

There was one last embarrassment in Hollywood for Elvis to endure; his 31st and final film, shot during March and April of 1969. It sank almost without a bubble to the surface, and its one merit was the presence of Mary Tyler Moore, soon to be a star in her own right with her TV show.

But the fact that his Hollywood days were over couldn't have mattered less to Elvis. Resurrected and newly adored as a singer, he was back on top of the world and about to inhabit a new stratosphere called Las Vegas. The King was climbing up to his throne again.

Parker had been busy negotiating a contract for Elvis to play at the International Hotel in Vegas, and he'd come away with a deal for $100,000 per week for twice-nightly performances over four weeks. It would be a singing marathon the like of which Elvis had never encountered. Elvis would have liked Scotty, D. J. and the Jordanaires to be part of his gospel backup, but they were already booked elsewhere and were not prepared to let others down whilst also accepting a salary cut from the Colonel. Everyone involved felt slightly betrayed by the others.

Elvis stood up to the Colonel again and again with his choice of musicians; accused of being profligate, Elvis countered that the stage needed to be filled, and after many days of auditions, his choice fell on Sweet Inspirations, a soul group of three women including Whitney Houston's mother Cissy. Instead of the Jordanaires, he would now be backed by the Imperials and

65

a thirty-five-piece string and brass orchestra. From a list of some fifty songs that he rehearsed, he was going to show the Americans the entire range of his musical tastes; the big ballads, the gospel, the blues, the rock and the country.

When the big day arrived, the 31st of July 1969, Elvis was riddled with nerves as usual, pacing up-and-down backstage. The audience was like a who's who of show business, from Burt Bacharach and Angie Dickinson to Pat Boone, Shirley Bassey and Fats Domino and included his old mentor, Sam Phillips.

Having slipped onto the stage without introduction, he was given a standing ovation by the 2,200-strong audience, and without saying a word to the audience, he launched into 'Blue Suede Shoes', and from then on Elvis could not lose.

"The lad just got out there, wrapped his lean torso around a guitar and hammered out song after song, stopping from time to time to readjust his anatomy", enthused one reviewer and the others were no less appreciative, although the Las Vegas Sun felt that Elvis the movie hero hadn't really pushed himself to earn the standing ovation from the fans and invited guests that he was given at the end of his one-hour show. There was a *"... pounding, ear aching sameness to many of Presley's songs. As far as the throng was concerned, however, Elvis could do no harm that night."*

Ending the show with 'Can't Help Falling in Love', the new slimmer Elvis would say that that night had been one of the most exciting of his entire life.

The Hotel management was very happy, too, so happy, in fact, that they were picking up the option for February and August appearances there for another five years at $1,000,000 per year. The lad certainly had staying power as

Newsweek magazine commented.

And his star continued to shine; when the double album from Memphis to Vegas / from Vegas to Memphis was released, the song 'Suspicious Minds' went to the top of the charts. It brought a rather unfortunate double with it; it was his first US pop number one in over seven years; but there would be no more.

But when he returned in February 1970 for his next Vegas engagement, the success was as warm as it had been the first time. Recordings from the shows were released in the On Stage album.

Elvis thoroughly enjoyed that first reunion night with the International. He had added songs to the song list such as 'The Wonder of You', which then became another hit single for him, reaching number one in the UK, and it was three in the morning before his 'one-hour' midnight show ended.

Elvis was also booked to appear at the Houston Astrodome in late February, when he performed six shows to record-breaking audience numbers.

This show would also go down in history for another rather less happy reason. Someone demanded $50,000 from the singer or he would kill him.

Threats to Elvis were not a rarity, although many of them would have been kept from him. This one wasn't, and with the FBI stepping up their presence for the two follow-up shows, Elvis went on stage with a .45 pistol secreted in his waistband, and his right boot contained a Derringer.

The incident only served to bring him closer to the establishment and the comfort of authority and especially the police. To the fiercely patriotic Elvis, the 60s hippies and their drug-fuelled subculture were a long-haired

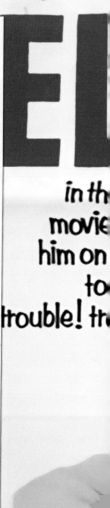

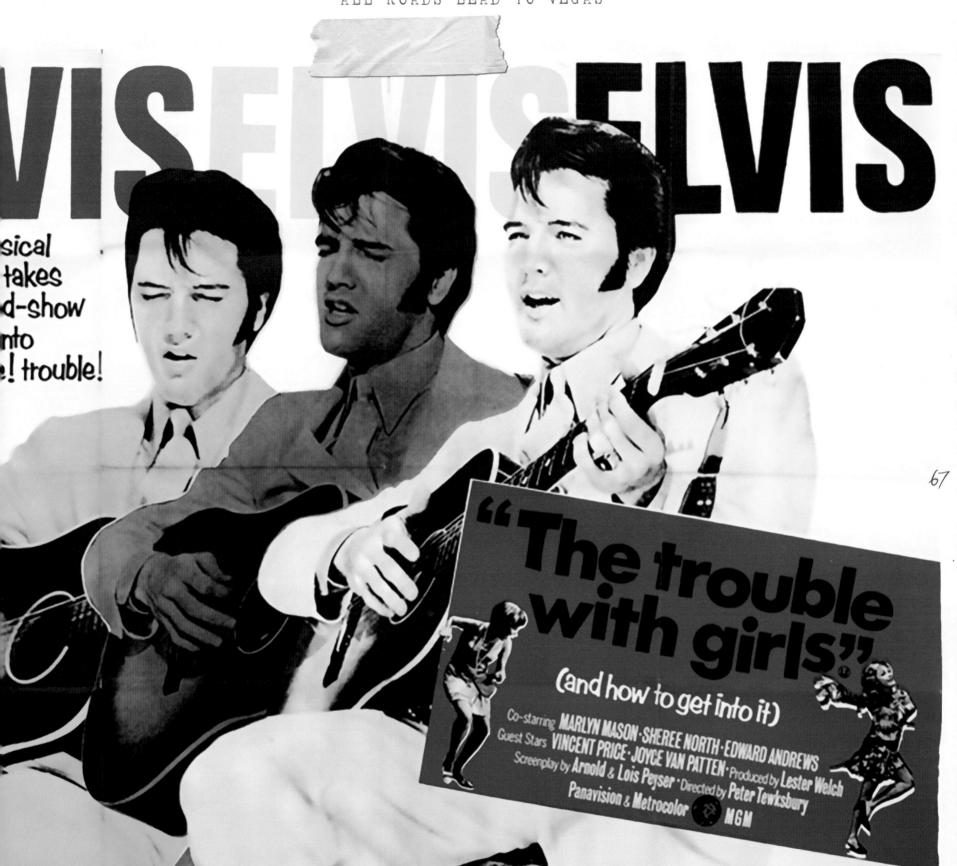

67

1969 The Trouble with Girls British Quad Movie Poster

threat, the burning of the American flag and anti-war sentiments or dubbing police 'pigs' outraged him. After all, he was an avid collector of police force badges, and uniforms had always appealed to him.

Elvis had always enjoyed wearing extravagant clothing; he'd even endured the mockery of his schoolmates with his sideburns and colourful outfits. On stage, he was now clad in a jumpsuit, and his white jumpsuit was a piece of clothing that would become his trademark. As time went on, it would acquire decorations of rhinestones and a superhero cape, extravagances for which Elvis would be known from then on.

Although fans screamed even if they had merely glanced at his ostentatious outline, Priscilla saw the signs of something less than healthy; it was, she found, the outward cry for help of a little boy lost and craving attention – and unknowingly, help. Help he would never receive and never ask for. Elvis the King never asked for anything.

He didn't need to ask for attention from his female admirers, legions of them, ready to smile, to flirt, to laugh at his jokes and to sleep with him. They all made Priscilla seem rather pale in comparison. The couple had little in common except religion; but music was his life, and when he wanted to talk music it would have to be with his fellow musicians or the girls from Sweet Inspirations. They made him laugh and he loved that. He loved women. He lied to Priscilla about his relations with other women. Did he love Priscilla? He never made love to her; his nightly sleeping pill put paid to that anyway, even if he'd wanted to, causing Priscilla to feel increasingly out on a limb and on her own. Elvis seemed to have made her a substitute Gladys, and she filled the role perfectly, even dicing his meat for him. But then he was away again in Los Angeles or elsewhere, partying and chasing girls while she looked after little Lisa Marie at home.

He did take her to Hawaii when he was at a loose end after his August in Vegas stint. It wasn't for her benefit, of course, the entire entourage went with them. When they moved on to the Bahamas, the strains on the relationship broke the bonds and led to arguments.

Following recording sessions in Nashville, Elvis was back in Vegas again in August 1970. With country "*put on the back burner, and soul and R&B left in Memphis*", as one music critic commented, Elvis was turning out "*very classy, very clean white pop*"; it was perfect fare for the Las Vegas visitors, and ensured the steady flow of money. MGM cameras filmed both the rehearsals and the show to produce a documentary; Elvis: That's the Way It Is. It was time to cash in on the Elvis phenomenon once more, and the album Elvis Country – 12 songs from the 35 that the five-day Nashville sessions had produced – was also issued that year alongside several others. Quality, as always with the Colonel, was of secondary importance to quantity as long as it brought in the money, and Elvis didn't complain. His extravagance worked to Parker's advantage; Elvis's money passed through the revolving door of his desires on a larger property in the Los Angeles, Holmby Hills area replete with a new Mercedes for himself and a new car for Vernon to sit beside the snowmobiles. The spending didn't end there, of course. Jewellery had always been a symbol of wealth and now $10,000 for a gold and bejewelled belt was not too much. And the entourage needed bracelets of gold, too, and silver pendants, as befitted Elvis's circle.

And then there were the guns.

Guns had always found their way to him as though he were magnetic. Since the threats against his life, he carried one in each boot on stage, and all the guys around him were licensed to bear arms, too. Gold was just about good enough to adorn his Colt and Baretta handles. Guns littered the house, and a Tommy gun could be fired by Elvis to express his

Backstage on the opening night of his comeback engagement at the Caesar's Palace Hotel in Las Vegas, 1970

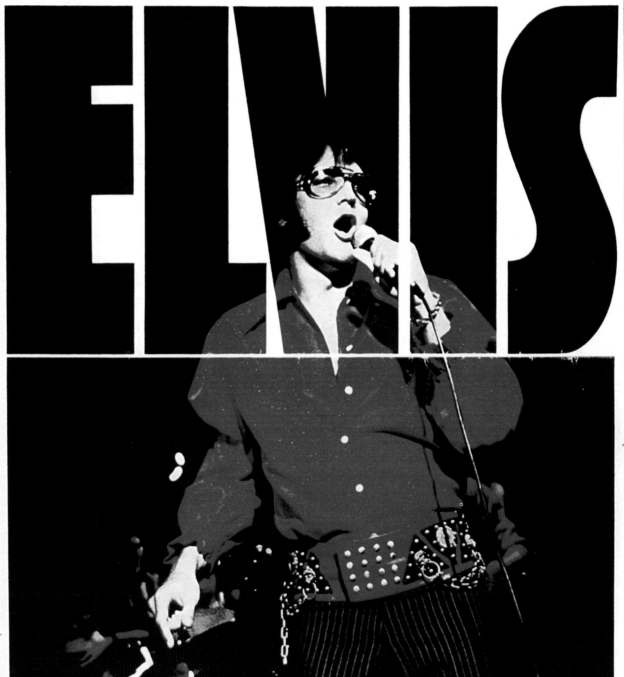

69

Elvis Presley during a press conference after his first performance at the International Hotel in Las Vegas, Nevada on August 1, 1969

Metro-Goldwyn-Mayer présente ELVIS PRESLEY
"THAT'S THE WAY IT IS" réalisation DENIS SANDERS
PANAVISION® • METROCOLOR®

MGM

Film poster for That's The Way It Is

displeasure at something as harmless as a toilet bowl. Tens of thousands of dollars could disappear in a night's shopping at a gun store, and not only Vernon and Priscilla were worried about the star's profligacy; Parker was frustrated, too.

There was a deeper need, a deeper fear, a deep patriotism in Elvis that those guns revealed; his obsession with all things connected with the police revealed another side of him as well; his longing for the order that they represented, and he collected police badges like sweets, hoarding them each time he was presented with another on his tours across country.

Never was he prouder than when he was awarded a gold deputy sheriff badge by the chief of police in Huston, or when he was awarded another deputy sheriff badge in Tennessee in late 1970; or the honorary Denver police badge and the commissioner's badge in Los Angeles; in his favourite colour again; gold. That deserved a donation, which made his bank account $7000 lighter.

When September the 7th rolled around, Elvis was off on his first concert tours since 1958, which took place mostly in the south, for one week, followed by one more week along the West Coast in November.

It was then that one of the stranger incidents in his life occurred, engineered by himself this time, not the Colonel. It was spurred by one of those arguments with his family about money. He railed at Vernon, and he railed at his wife. His wife? It was hardly a marriage anymore, was it? Anyway. His money, his choices, not theirs, not Parker's. His.

Enraged and needing to escape the noose, Elvis stormed out of the house and took off in his car down Highway 51. He had no idea where he was going; a girl in Washington D. C. perhaps. Leaving the car at the airport in Memphis, he was soon on a plane out of the state.

Once in Washington, his plan to see the girl had become superseded by another, more exciting one after the search for her proved difficult. Superseded by two plans, to be more exact. Another police badge from the Bureau of Narcotics and Dangerous drugs would fit into his collection beautifully.

He was on his way across the country when the second plan formed.

The badge would be his in an instant if he could enlist the support of the President of the United States; as would be his enrolment as a federal drug agent. And as Elvis always got what he wanted, there was no doubt that this plan would come to fruition, too.

A letter of introduction was needed, which he wrote whilst still in the air on five pages of American Airlines stationery and which is now in the National Archive. Unwittingly, in his writing he had shown a conflicted man, whose inner self was raging in a *river of turmoil*, as one handwriting expert described it. He had also proven once and for all that here was no rock 'n' roll rebel, more of a sheep in wolf's clothing.

The star wrote to the president:

Dear Mr. President.

First, I would like to introduce myself. I am Elvis Presley and admire you and have great respect for your office. I talked to Vice President Agnew in Palm Springs three weeks ago and expressed my concern for our country. The drug culture, the hippie elements, the SDS, Black Panthers, etc. do not consider me as their enemy or as they call it the establishment. I call it America and I love it. Sir, I can

AmericanAirlines

In Flight…

Altitude; ①

Location;

Dear Mr. President.

First I would like to introduce myself. I am Elvis Presley and admire you and Have Great Respect for your office. I talked to Vice President Agnew in Palm Springs 3 weeks and expressed my concern for our country. The Drug Culture, The Hippie Elements, the SDS, Black Panthers, etc do not consider me as their enemy or as they call it the Establishment. I call it america and

AmericanAirlines

In Flight…

Altitude; ②

Location;

I Love it. Sir I can and will be of any Service that I can to help the country out. I have no concern or Motives other than helping the country out. So I wish not to be given a title or an appointed Position, I can and will do more good if I were made a Federal agent at Large, and I will help out by doing it my way through my communications with people of all ages. First and Foremost I am an entertainer but All I need is the Federal credentials. I am on this Plane with

AmericanAirlines

In Flight…

Altitude; ③

Location;

Sen. George Murphy and We have been discussing the problems that our Country is faced with. So I am Staying at the Washington Hotel Room 505-506-507. I have 2 men who work with me by the name of Jerry Schilling and Sonny West. I am registered under the name of Jon Burrows. I will be here for as long as it takes to get the credentials of a Federal agent. I have done an in depth study of Drug abuse and Communist Brainwashing

71

AmericanAirlines

In Flight…

Altitude; 4

Location;

Techniques and I am right in the middle of the whole thing, where I can and will do the most good I am Glad to help just so long as it is kept very Private. You can have your staff or whomever call me anytime today, tonight or Tomorrow I was nominated this coming year one of America's Ten most outstanding young men. That will be in January 18 in my Home Town of Memphis Tenn. I am sending you the short autobiography about myself so you can better understand this

AmericanAirlines

In Flight…

Altitude; 5

Location;

~~approach~~

approach. I would Love to meet you just to say hello if you're not to Busy.

Respectfully

Elvis Presley

P.S. I believe that you Sir were one of the Top Ten Outstanding Men of america also.

I have a personal gift for you also which I would like to present to you and you can accept it or I will keep it for you until you can take it.

Written on American Airlines stationery, the five-page letter requested a meeting with President Nixon. Presley intended to present the President with a gift of a World War II-era pistol and obtain for himself the credentials of a federal agent in the war on drugs and will be of any service that I can to help the country out. I have no concern or motives other than helping the country out.

So I wish not to be given a title or an appointed position. I can and will do more good if I were made a Federal Agent at Large and I will help out by doing it my way through my communications with people of all ages. First and foremost, I am an entertainer, but all I need is the Federal credentials. I am on this plane with Senator George Murphy and we have been discussing the problems that our country is faced with.

Sir, I am staying at the Washington Hotel, Room 505-506-507. I have two men who work with me by the name of Jerry Schilling and Sonny West. I am registered under the name of Jon Burrows. I will be here for as long as it takes to get the credentials of a Federal Agent. I have done an in-depth study of drug abuse and Communist brainwashing techniques and I am right in the middle of the whole thing where I can and will do the most good.

I am glad to help just so long as it is kept very private. You can have your staff or whomever call me anytime today, tonight, or tomorrow. I was nominated this coming year one of America's Ten Most Outstanding Young Men. That will be in January 18 in my home town of Memphis, Tennessee. I am sending you the short autobiography about myself so you can better understand this approach. I would love to meet you just to say hello if you're not too busy.

Respectfully,
Elvis Presley
P. S. I believe that you, Sir, were one of the Top Ten Outstanding Men of America also.

I have a personal gift for you which I would like to present to you and you can accept it or I will keep it for you until you can take it.

Mr. President
These are all my PVT numbers... (Elvis lists them).

WASHINGTON HOTEL PHONE ME : 85900 Room 505-506. Under the name of Jon Burrows
PRIVATE AND CONFIDENTIAL
Attn. President Nixon
via Sen. George Murphy.
from

Elvis Presley.

In the light of Presley's own extensive drug use, it was an even more extraordinary letter and more proof of his self-deception; and of his self-image as a special person.

His plane landed at about 6.30 in the morning of December the 21st 1970, and Elvis took his letter in a limo straight to the northwest gate of the White House. Presley intended to present the president with a gift of a World War II-era pistol.

Then he drove to get his badge from the Bureau. They refused to give him one. But by 12 noon, the call from the White House had arrived. The president would see him at 12.30.

Attired in a flared jumpsuit with a large gold belt buckle and sunglasses - the pearl-handled Colt .45 pistol from his private collection, his gift for the president had been removed by secret service guards beforehand - Elvis walked into the Oval Office to shake hands with Richard Nixon.

Elvis was relaxed, as opposed to Nixon, who later said that the encounter had been "uncomfortable", as he expounded on his mission. Which was to show his gratitude for the rewards from the American Dream that had come his way and help counter the influence of the drug and hippy world

December 31, 1970

Dear Mr. Presley:

It was a pleasure to meet with you in my office
recently, and I want you to know once again how
much I appreciate your thoughtfulness in giving
me the commemorative World War II Colt 45
pistol, encased in the handsome wooden chest.
You were particularly kind to remember me
with this impressive gift, as well as your family
photographs, and I am delighted to have them for
my collection of special mementos.

With my best wishes to you, Mrs. Presley, and
to your daughter, Lisa, for a happy and peaceful
1971,

Sincerely,

RICHARD NIXON

Mr. Elvis Presley
Box 417
Madison, Tennessee 37115

RN/lf/cf/cf   gift

as represented by the Beatles or Jane Fonda that, as he saw it,
threatened to toxify American youth. (Paul McCartney said that
he felt "*betrayed*" when he eventually learned of the encounter.)
His status, Elvis thought, made him eminently suited to the task
of wearing the badge of a narcotics agent to send the message
to the country's vulnerable youngsters. Nixon thought so, too,
and the BNDD badge was granted to a tearful and elated Presley,
who also persuaded the president to give cufflinks with the
presidential seal to the two men who had accompanied him to
Washington; Jerry Schilling and Sonny West; and their wives
could look forward to presidential pins, too.

Elvis emerged into the daylight triumphant. It had been a bizarre
event, captured by White House cameras, one that filled Elvis's
every waking hour over the whole of the Christmas period.

Now he had to attend to the symbols of his new office, so money was
thrown at a police radio and a blue light for his car, handcuffs

Backstage in a concert venue, 1970

and, of course, guns suitable for a federal agent.

And the rewards for being Elvis kept coming. He was to receive one of America's Ten Outstanding Young Men of the Year awards, could boast sell-out audiences and now he had been granted an audience with the president; The King was truly the King.

Elvis accepted his Jaycee award (U. S. Junior Chamber of Commerce) in a ceremony on the 16th of January the following year. He worked on his speech, and "... *stood in the wings at the auditorium in Memphis... and admitted he was terrified*". "*He was*" said a reporter, "*perspiring profusely and his head was hanging low as he awaited his turn on stage as one of the United States Jaycees Ten Outstanding Young Men of America for 1970.*"

But Elvis knew that the sell by date for "*Those whom the Gods love*" came around rapidly. He was to receive the first intimations of mortality following his stint at the International in Vegas in February – an obligation that was beginning to bore him – after which he began recording in Nashville.

Finding that his eyes were stinging painfully during the recording sessions, even forcing him to leave the recording studio, he went to see a doctor and received the diagnosis of secondary glaucoma. In a world that revolved around Elvis, this news that he was as human as everyone else frightened the singer, and although follow up examinations removed the fear that he was going blind, and indicated that the stinging might possibly have come from the dye in his eyebrows, he was, nonetheless, subjected to injections of cortisone into his eyeballs; without anaesthetic. The King and his sunglasses and would be inseparable from then on.

During the sessions, Elvis also recorded some Gordon Lightfoot songs, prompting Lightfoot to praise his version of 'Early Morning Rain' as the best he had ever heard. Unlike Chris Kristofferson, whose song 'Help Me Make It through the Night' Elvis also moulded to his style; Kristofferson was unimpressed. That reaction seemed to throw light on Elvis's

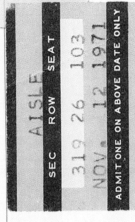

increasingly lax attitude towards his work at the time.

According to one critic, "*...the one real highlight*" of one of the 1971 sessions were the recordings of "*I Will Be True*", "*It's Still Here*" and "*I'll Take You Home Again, Kathleen*". Elvis had recorded these sitting alone at the piano in the empty recording studio. They seemed to contain the man behind the glittering facade, his neediness, his loneliness, his yearning, his nostalgia. And they were infused with the emotional honesty that Elvis was finding it more and more difficult to communicate in his work.

He felt dissatisfied with what he was doing. There would be no hit single that Christmas, which was a disappointment, even though his Christmas album itself did well enough. One of the problems stemmed from singing in the dry Nevada air twice nightly. Elvis's velvety voice had become strained, its flexibility compromised, its nuances flattened, so that low and high notes became coarse and best avoided. And gone was the flair, the devil-may-care rebellion that his warm tones had displayed during the rock 'n' roll years; he had already settled into the middle-of-the-road, easy listening for Las Vegas ears, which he combined with sartorial opulence in a victory for show over substance. He had become, by 1971, as much of an institution to see on the tourist trail as the Grand Canyon or the trolley cars in San Francisco.

Adding Lake Tahoe to his Vegas concerts, he then toured the country, revolving between concerts and girlfriends, home, wife and hearth.

74

Except that, home, wife, hearth and child were becoming increasingly distanced from him. He was no longer in love with Priscilla; it was more the idea of a stable home life that he wanted to keep upright, one that was ready for him when he needed it with all the people in it that he liked, one that allowed him the freedom to do what he wanted outside of it; a sterile environment in which resided his illusions of family life. Illusions, because Priscilla was no longer the shy teenager afraid of approaching his entourage for fear of his temper tantrums. They were now on her side covering her tracks, because she was having an affair of her own. Nor was it the first time; she'd also had a brief affair with her dance instructor in 1968.

"*He had mentioned to me before*", wrote Priscilla later about her husband, "*... that he had never been able to make love to a woman who had a child*", and his disinterest in her physically caused her much heartache, and no doubt their dysfunctional sex life was partly to blame for her being pushed her over the edge, despite her continued love for the singer.

Priscilla had taken up karate, a sport that Elvis pursued keenly, taking lessons from a karate instructor she had met at a karate Championship in 1968 in Hawaii and then again backstage at one of Elvis's concerts in 1972. His name was Mike Stone. She was having an affair with him. She wanted a divorce.

Elvis might have suspected if he had thought about it at all that his wife was not sitting at home waiting for him. But he was self-absorbed; other people's problems were not his. And it's indicative of the man living in his bubble,

that what he claimed for himself he regarded as 'betrayal' in others. Nothing illustrated this more succinctly than his relationship with Joyce Bova, the girl with whom he had since become entangled again after he had flown to Washington to try and see her. Writing after the event, Joyce Bova maintained that Elvis had wanted to entice her to continue their secret romance and ask her forgiveness for mistreating her. "*He was egocentric*", she recalled, although the most beautiful man that she had ever met.

But then, Bova became pregnant, although she soon sought an abortion. Unbeknownst to Elvis. Elvis even spoke about Joyce moving to Graceland; life with Priscilla wasn't going so smoothly.

Yet, when the axe fell just before New Year of 1972, it was a "*blow from which he never recovered*", according to Joe Moscheo of the Imperials, which sent Presley into a depression.

She was leaving him, Priscilla told him; she no longer loved him. She was taking Lisa Marie and flying back to Los Angeles. They agreed to keep news of the separation away from the press for the sake of their little girl.

The man who thought that he was the image he saw whenever he looked in the mirror, which he did a great deal, had fallen into the vacuum he himself had created. Now he could no longer ignore the fact that he had fallen far short of the illusion he had projected onto the world. When asked by a reporter at a press conference later in 1972 about his image, he replied, "*Well, the human being is one thing. The image is another. It's very hard to live up to an image.*" A paternity order seemed to testify to that, even though blood tests eventually cleared him.

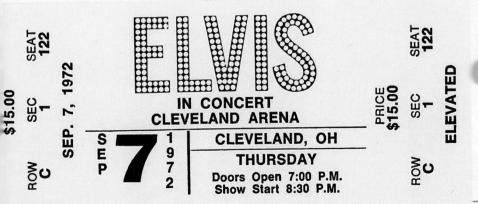

"ELVIS HAS LEFT THE BUILDING"

The 1970s had begun badly for Elvis's personal life, and the years to come, and there were not many of them left, would prove to be difficult ones.

His professional life was as buoyant as it had ever been, even though nationwide tours and the concerts in Las Vegas repeated like gong strokes had seen him fall into routine and boredom. In April 1972, MGM filmed Elvis for another documentary; Elvis on Tour. It went on to win the Golden Globe for Best Documentary Film 1972. He would also win a second Grammy Award for the gospel album He Touched Me, for the Best Inspirational Performance.

One of the only highlights whilst on tour in the summer of 1972 was the excitement he experienced when he played four shows in Madison Square Garden in New York, all of them sold out, making Elvis the first performer ever to achieve those heights. Just those four shows grossed $730,000.

Show business, as Elvis noted, was all about image, and the image of Elvis in floral shirts, long hair and his bejewelled gold belt, had now become iconic in America, Elvis the epitome of the American rags to gaudy riches dream. The American Idol was happy to give what the paying public wanted, and both they and the press critics loaded praise upon him for his shows. Three million of them bought the live album of his New York performance. Yet Presley was beginning to understand that the image only had meaning when supported by strong personal life. Joyce too, had fled the drug-ridden, temperamental and bizarre life with the singer for a more sane world, to be replaced with Linda Thompson, Presley's new girlfriend, a

former Memphis beauty queen and a songwriter, who had now moved in with him, having taken up residence shortly after Priscilla and Lisa Marie moved on. Having met Elvis in Memphis on July the 6th 1972, "*The man I absolutely adored with all of my heart and soul*", she wrote, they spent nearly all of their time together in a relationship that would endure for almost five years. What did she do right? She replaced his mother Gladys, as Elvis's nickname for her, "*mommy*", plainly shows and took care of him. As a Southern Baptist, she was willing to read the Bible with him, and he was willing to wait to have a sexual relationship with her until she was ready. Rather ironic in view of his amorous sideshows; which Linda turned a blind eye to. The entourage liked her because she made the house tyrant happy. And she was glamorous. That was a prerequisite, and she looked glamorous in the clothes that he now lavished upon her as he had done upon Priscilla.

Nonetheless, it was still only the resplendent, over-the-top image that the fans adored; but what of the real Elvis? Had they truly known him, what would they think of him? He often wondered.

Despite the fact that Linda Thompson was now a feature in his life, he still could not resist the charms of other women and girls, the best looking of whom the boys would gather up for him from the queues outside the venues.

Beauty Queens had always attracted him and now another

Elvis Presley performing live onstage at the 'Aloha from Hawaii' concert, wearing a white jumpsuit

Poster for Elvis On Tour

one hove up onto the horizon; her name was Cybill Shepherd. She was starring in a movie and singularly unimpressed by his attempts to win her over with his wealth and fame. She stayed for a while and took care of the man-child, but eventually she could no longer put up with his dependence on drugs. A dependence that Elvis was easily able to deny to himself in his distorted world, because his were prescription drugs not 'street' drugs.

Even through his own self-absorption, Elvis could not fail to notice that a change had come about in Tom Parker's life as well. The man whose every waking, probably sleeping hour had revolved around the promotion of the magic money tree known as Elvis Presley, whose natural inclination was to gather money in not to spend it – he lived a quiet and unpretentious life with his wife Marie, devoid of any showbiz nonsense – had been spending an increasing amount of time at the tables in Las Vegas. His occasional betting turned into an obsession that meant that he was Elvis's equal in spending lavish amounts of money, which now flowed out of both men's pockets as quickly as it flowed in. It was just as well that the Presley magic was bringing in waterfalls of money, because Parker's Vegas habit, and his habit of losing, did not bode well for the future of either man. Quick to criticise Elvis for his spending profligacy, he was equally quick to forbid criticism of his own.

The big event in Elvis's life in 1973 was, Elvis: Aloha from Hawaii. It would be the first satellite transmission of a music concert ever, and RCA and NBC had teamed up to amass an audience of up to 1.5 billion when it was broadcast on January the 14th 1973, just a few days after Elvis's 38th birthday.

Terrified and flattered to be asked, he was fired up for this event, and when director Marty Pasetta advised him that he needed to lose weight, he agreed easily. Weight was a touchy subject and never spoken about amongst the entourage unless Elvis mentioned it first. He went on a crash diet, restricting himself to just 500 calories a day for two weeks to look his best for the world and do justice to his white, ornate jumpsuit and the American eagle that would emblazon his cape, embroidered and studded with jewels of glass. This costume, more than any other, would fix the flamboyant Elvis image in the memories of audiences around the world.

The benefit concert rehearsals had been filmed, just in case any hitches might arise on the day of the actual performances; included in the song list were evergreens such as 'My Way', 'Blue Suede Shoes', 'I'm So Lonesome I Could Cry', 'Hound Dog' and 'Can't Help Falling in Love'.

Elvis had reached the pinnacle of his career with this show, and everyone who was close to him was in Hawaii to watch. The pressure was enormous, and he succumbed to a vitamin injection with amphetamines before he went on. It was the start of another worrying period in his life.

After the thrill of Hawaii, it was back to the conveyor belt in Las Vegas, where the International had become the Las Vegas Hilton. One night he lost his voice and had to abandon the stage. He missed three shows and had to drag himself through the remainder of his engagements. Stimulants before the show, sedatives after the show to keep the fears and the sleepless nights at bay, kept him going. His anxieties were not eased when four over-enthusiastic fans leapt onto the stage during one midnight show to be tackled by security and Elvis himself, whose karate skills enabled him to dispense with one of them. Paranoid, he thought that Mike Stone had sent them to kill him and raged to an astonished audience. Never before had he allowed his personal feelings to be heard in public, but made unstable by pills, he continued to rage for days afterwards. He even tried to get his friend Red, now reconciled with the singer, to shoot Mike Stone,

Elvis Presley holds a press conference at the Las Vegas Hilton Hotel to announce his upcoming concert 'Aloha from Hawaii'

Performing live onstage, 1975

79

who had, as Elvis saw it, stolen his wife and was trying to ruin his life. Linda was terrified and in tears, doctors administered sedatives. Fortunately for everybody, the cloud eventually passed and Elvis was content to *"Just leave it for now."*

Elvis was now a slave to his prescription drugs; he knew them all and what they could do for him, the Valium, Seconal, Demerol and Nembutal amongst others, all of which compliant doctors could acquire for him. Everyone around him was worried, no one could, or wanted to, really stand up to Elvis's addiction. Although Red and Sonny tried.

Elvis overdosed on barbiturates twice in 1973; the first time left him in a coma for three days. As the year drew to an end after his divorce, he was hospitalised, suffering from the effects of a Demerol addiction and a bleeding ulcer caused by cortisone. Gone was the svelte Singer of

SPOKANE COLISEUM
BOONE & HOWARD · SPOKANE, WASHINGTON

SATURDAY EVE. 8:00 P.M.

APRIL
28
1973

RCA RECORD TOURS
— PRESENTS —
ELVIS

EST. PR. $4.76
CITY TAX .24 $5.00
TOTAL

ADMIT ONE. Good this date only
NO REFUNDS

10 M 12
UPPER CONCOURSE

GOOD ONLY
SATURDAY EVE.
APRIL
28
1973

10 M 12
SEC. ROW SEAT
UPPER CONCOURSE $5.00
SPOKANE COLISEUM

Hawaii; now he was described as having a gut, and on one occasion in Maryland, he fell out of his limousine and slurred his way through a concert.

Had Elvis not been so wrapped up in his own world and increasing drug problems, he might have seen through Parker's asset grab when Parker presented him with an RCA deal; $5.4 million for the rights to more than 650 recordings. An appalling deal – except for Parker, who would take half for himself leaving Presley with just one quarter after taxes. Parker needed to service his gambling debts, after all.

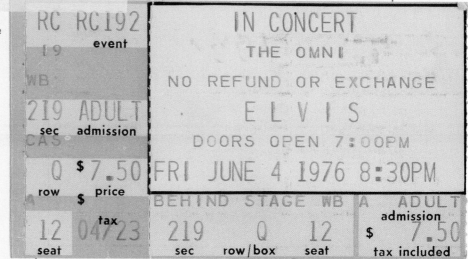

So Elvis was soon back out on tour again in the relentless quest to fund his lifestyle and the Colonel's suffering bank account. RCA insisted he returned to the recording studio in July, where he produced not one probable hit tune, and then simply left the studio when his favourite microphone couldn't be found. Afterwards it was back to Las Vegas for more of the same routine.
He became careless in his stage show and involved in a furious row with the Colonel because of it. *"You're fired!"* Elvis yelled at him. Parker wanted $2 million from him. Elvis, presented with a world he knew nothing about – his bank accounts – caved in.

Money formed the central theme of another event in his life on October the 9th; the divorce settlement with Priscilla. $725,000 in cash plus monthly payments of $6000, adding up to $1,250,000. $1200 a month alimony for the next five years, $4000 a month for Lisa Marie's child-support. There was also 50% of the sale price of their house in Beverly Hills, plus 5% of stock in Elvis's music publishing business for her.

There was not much to brighten the forecast for 1974 either. February saw him back in Las Vegas, although on doctor's advice, he was now playing for just two weeks.

But there was no let up in the pace, because tours would fill up the months ahead, forty-five performances in five weeks, his existence fuelled by drugs, the performances notably lacking in energy. Unmotivated, overweight, he sang for the dollars, for the young girls, for the fame; music no longer interested him. There would be no studio recordings in 1974, and RCA's concerns were somewhat placated with a concert record; Elvis Recorded Live on Stage in Memphis from which his version of 'How Great Thou Art' would win Elvis his third and last competitive Grammy Award.

RCA had good reason to be nervous; Elvis was now indulging in monotonously endless ramblings between songs, throwing out whatever came into his mind from divorce to girlfriends, from drugs to health issues, proving that his indignant anger at being described as *"strung out"* on drugs was a hypocritical facade. The king's behaviour was out of control in tandem with his spending, one seeming to feed the other.

Before the end of the year he was back in the clinic for recuperation and as much of the longed-for sleep as he could get. The 'little helpers' had become more and more vital as the Colonel worked him, literally, down to the

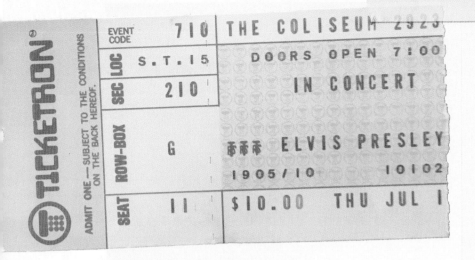

ground, squeezing him until every last coin had come clinking out.

Frightening mood swings and the frightening realisation that he was on a downward slide made him fear life without the drugs – to which liquid cocaine may now have been added – far more than the inevitable end point, the existence of which could always be denied.

1975 would see Elvis celebrate his 40th birthday; if celebrate was the right word. With the press calling him fat and forty, his age brought on a mini midlife crisis. He was unused to criticism and anything but unconditional adoration. What were the fans thinking about him now that he was entering middle age, and would they remain faithful? Ignoring the celebrations prepared at Graceland, Elvis spent his birthday behind the gold-painted door of his bedroom.

The mirror in the bedroom was unkind; a facelift was needed, Elvis and plastic surgery being something about which there had been much speculation in the past, although Linda Thompson claimed that his 40th-birthday-year procedure was the "*extent of his plastic surgery*".

Another stay in hospital followed, and when Vernon

suffered a heart attack on the 5th of February, he and Elvis – admitted after breathing problems – were in rooms next to one another. Elvis's attempt to dry out was thwarted by illicit deliveries from family, staff, and friends. But the stay brought about a four-month rest from work, the longest of his career.

Nothing could ease the torment in his mind, however, his erratic behaviour, his frustrated bouts of shooting in hotel rooms, his expensive splurges – on 14 Cadillacs for the entourage, planes, gifts, jewellery for friends and Linda – nor stop his insults directed at his fellow musicians and girlfriends. Friends left never to return. The man who had always felt alone was doing his absolute best to make that condition as intense as possible; Linda's patience, too, was exhausted.

Elvis's gold mine, his voice, was seriously depleted; gone the delicate top notes and the chocolate dark low tones. Recording had become a chore to be avoided, and in February 1976, RCA would have to resort to bringing the studio to him so that they could squeeze a song from him. And he did make the effort, descending from his bedroom to the 'Jungle Room' to record songs that had to be lowered in pitch to accommodate his restricted range. Gone was the soaring tenor of his youth to be replaced by a faltering baritone.

Amongst songs such as 'Girl of my Best Friend', 'Moody Blue', 'For the Heart' and 'I'll Never Fall in Love Again', and the last song that Elvis ever recorded, 'He'll Have To Go', was 'Hurt', described by one reviewer as an "*apocalyptic attack*" on the classic soul number, and his most critically acclaimed song of the period.

Then the road claimed him.

The applause was as huge as ever, but the decline was now

81

undeniable, critics unpitying; lyrics to his favourite songs refused to come leaving the Sweet Inspirations to cover for him. Physically he had to stop singing during concerts to get his breath back. He needed to do the same with his life, too, but there was no one to help. No Gladys. He wouldn't listen to anyone else.

It was almost symbolic of the circus closing down when he allowed himself to be persuaded by Vernon to fire Red and Sonny for being too forceful with fans. Or was it their outspoken attitude against Elvis's drug use that damned them? Unwilling to face his long-time friends himself, he had them fired.

Devastated, Red's revenge was to phone Elvis for a heartfelt chat and have the call recorded for the press, an action that left Elvis in tears and Red with a sense of guilt. Even though Red and Sonny had agreed a book deal to spill the beans on their years with the King. They rejected an offer of $50,000 from Elvis's side not to go ahead with the book.

His health continued to deteriorate, but there could be no let up in the number of concert dates. Throughout 1976, Elvis performed in one tour after another, the quality of his shows a long way from his peak years. Divorce settlements, personal extravagance, largesse distributed to all and sundry, and the upkeep of his houses saw to that. As did Parker, who needed the Elvis cash cow to keep producing to feed his own debts and gambling addiction. It was a treadmill. The songs were heard, but – to hijack a phrase that was fed to waiting fans to encourage them to go home –

Elvis had left the building.

Elvis Presley tosses a nylon scarf into the waiting hands of the fans at a concert in the Providence Civic Center, Providence, Rhode Island

83

"FORGET ME NEVER"

Linda had left him.

After almost five years, the relationship had become more unstable as the months passed and, as usual, his relationships with other women, platonic as they might have been, caused problems between Elvis and Linda. Patience finally exhausted, she had found someone else to transfer her affections to.

Into this disintegrating mix, the boys in his entourage one day introduced the spice of a girl called Ginger Alden. The three Alden sisters were invited to Graceland, scrutinised by Elvis on his closed-circuit TV, and after chatting to them, he chose Ginger, who then spent most of the night with him – reading religious books and checking their suitability for one another in the Book of Numbers.

Elvis indifferently made the end of his relationship with Linda as ignominious as possible; on tour in San Francisco, he suggested Linda might take a break for a few days. She understood; a replacement had arrived. Childishly believing that he could still deceive the adult world around him, he told Linda that there was no other woman and that he still loved her. It was hurtful to be lied to, although Linda didn't believe him anyway. She left for a new life away from the neurosis; they would never meet again.

The high that Elvis gained from a new sexual victory was fleeting; Ginger was, more than twenty years younger than him and had no intention of succumbing to the solitary night-owl life that Linda has been forced into. His world seemed to have shrunk to his bedroom and his books on spiritualism. Despite the fact that he showered gifts upon her in a desperate attempt to keep her by his side at every moment he was free, she refused to follow his every command, preferring to be with her friends and sisters of her own age. Elvis's behaviour swung crazily, arcing between frightening anger, self-indulgent adoration, pleading, and a dictatorial iron fist. Elvis was soon writing notes to himself in the dead of night – cries for help; "*I wish there was someone who I could trust to talk to*", "*Help me Lord*", "*I feel so alone now*".

Even his most loyal fans were voicing their disillusionment, because his voice was often reduced to nothing more than a thin warble, his articulation as flabby and indistinct as his body. Concerned, his old friend Scotty watched from afar: "*The last time I saw him, I can't remember what the show was, where he had gained so much weight and I could tell there was something wrong but I didn't know what.*"

Parker drove him relentlessly on down the chute to the bottom. Touring continued on through the spring and the summer and two concerts were filmed for CBS, showing him to be just a pale shadow of his former self, drugged and bloated, the movements that had once sent fans into paroxysms of ecstasy nothing more than clumsy gestures. After a brief spell in hospital, he returned to face rows with Ginger, more touring, lawsuits, divorce payments, his father's ill-health; and in August would come the moment he had been dreading, the publication of Elvis: What Happened, revealing all that Red and Sonny had to tell.

When he went on stage in Indianapolis on the 26th of June 1977, many might have wondered how long he could keep beating the horse to keep the show rolling; few would have guessed that they had just witnessed his final public appearance. There was, after all, another tour planned in August.

Presley with his girlfriend Ginger Alden in March of 1977 in Hawaii

There were a few weeks of respite in Graceland; without Ginger, as he lay in bed reading the Bible or watching the Sunday morning evangelical preachers on one of his three televisions who failed to lift his depressed mood, and he stayed more or less permanently in his pyjamas. The world around him closed inexorably down; Parker, it had been discovered, was an illegal alien, a Dutchman. Now it suddenly made sense why the Colonel had never allowed Elvis to tour in Europe or even leave the country. Did it really matter?

For a while, there was a break in the gloom when Ginger arrived, as did little Lisa Marie on one of her visits. She brought out the best in her father – for as long as he was able to cope before his doctor's visit would bring more uppers and downers; strong painkillers and sleeping pills that would take him away from the cares of the world.

But one night, with Ginger sound asleep beside him, the pills weren't working.

The night wore on; he tinkled on the piano; how was he going to manage with a tour starting again if he couldn't sleep? More pills were brought to him, but he was still awake when Ginger woke up. Then he went into his bathroom with a book to read. It was the 16th of August 1977.

It was around 1.30 in the afternoon when Ginger opened the bathroom door. Elvis was lying face down on the floor.

AISLE
SEC ROW SEAT
8 BB 108
JUNE 26, 1977

IN CONCERT
ELVIS
MARKET SQUARE ARENA
JUNE **26** 1977
INDIANAPOLIS, IND.
– SUNDAY
Doors Open – 7:00 PM
SHOWTIME – 8:30 PM

THE Sun

HE WAS 42 AND ALONE

Wednesday, August 17, 1977   6p   TODAY'S TV PAGES 12 and 13

KING ELVIS DEAD

FAT AND FORTY . . . *One of the last pictures of rocking king Elvis Presley*

From ROSS WABY   in New York

ELVIS PRESLEY, the rock 'n' roll king who thrilled millions, died alone yesterday aged 42.

He was felled by a massive heart attack . . . and died in his mansion home before help could reach him.

Elvis, who had been ill for some time, was found by his road manager Joe Esposito.

Mr Esposito sent for an ambulance and tried to revive Elvis.

Then medical staff massaged the superstar's heart as the ambulance sped from his home in Memphis, Tennessee to the city's Baptist hospital.

FATHER

Elvis's personal doctor, George Nichopoulos, who was in the ambulance, kept imporing the singer: "Come on, Presley, breathe. Breathe for me."

Doctors then battled for half an hour before announcing that he was dead.

Dr Nichopoulos said later that he suspected a heart attack was the cause of death, but this could not be confirmed until a post mortem examination.

Big crowds gathered outside the hospital, where

A massive heart attack at mansion

The idol who had the whole world rocking
Pages 4 and 5

relatives after death was confirmed.

"I don't know why we are here— we're just paying our condolences," said a middle-aged woman who stood with a throng at the hospital gates

The sudden death will shock millions of Elvis fans world-wide.

But it was no surprise to those close to him.

For Elvis, the poor boy who became the world's highest paid performer, was the victim of his own phenominal success.

His millions enabled him to indulge his every whim, and that led to his undoing

food—hamburgers and soft drinks—became an addiction, as did his thirst for thrills and experiences . . . and drugs.

Elvis sought kicks with cars, motorcycles, women, parties, guns, pinball machines, pool tables and no timetable.

He liked to stay up late —all night if he was enjoying himself—surrounded by the cousins and bodyguards that comprised his "Memphis Mafia."

DRUGS

To keep his body going as he sated himself, he turned more and more to drugs.

Red West, a bodyguard, said recently: "He takes pills to go to sleep, he takes pills to get up, he takes pills to go to the lavatory, and he takes pills to stop

Something had frightened him whilst he was sitting on the toilet; he had stood up, stumbled a few steps, fallen down, and unable to right himself or breathe properly had given in to the inevitable. His face was discoloured and swollen.

Elvis was dead.

Ambulances arrived and his doctor. Within seven minutes Elvis was in the Baptist Memorial Hospital in Memphis, but he had died long before.

His death can hardly have surprised those closest to him and many who had observed his decline over several years. Ten different drugs were found in his system when he died. He'd had also been known to take Dilaudid, Percodan, Placidyl, Dexedrine, Biphetamine, Tiunal, Desbutal, Escatrol, Amytal, Quaaludes, Carbrital, Seconal, Methadone, and Ritalin.

Vernon insisted that Elvis would have wished his fans to see him at Graceland one last time, and so, before the funeral, clad in a white suit in his coffin, Elvis was brought back to Graceland, the gates were opened, and the fans streamed past their idol, thousands disappointed when the gates closed again some three-and-a-half hours later.

On the 18th of August, Elvis's funeral was held at Graceland, before he was brought to Forest Hill Cemetery. Vernon said his final words to him "*Daddy will be with you soon*", and Elvis was laid to rest beside his mother.

(But after an attempted break-in by grave robbers, Elvis was reinterred at Graceland in October 1977. Vernon died two years later.)

Elvis had left everything he owned to Lisa Marie to be inherited at the age of 25.

The show for all the family was over.

87

20 THINGS YOU NEED TO KNOW ABOUT
ELVIS PRESLEY

Singer, movie star and cultural icon Elvis Presley was one of the most influential musicians of the 20th century. He is known as the King of Rock and Roll, the musical genre which he popularised and brought into the mainstream during the 1950s.

It is hard to overstate his impact on popular culture of the time. His talent and good looks – together with sexualised performances which scandalised mid-50s America – made him the world's first rock and roll superstar. He became a movie star and, later, a veteran of the Las Vegas 'residency'.

Years after his untimely death from a heart attack on August 16, 1977 aged just 42, he remains the best-selling solo artist in the history of recorded music, and second only to The Beatles overall, with record sales of over 250 million. He won three competitive Grammy awards during his career and the Grammy Lifetime Achievement Award when he was 36, as well as being inducted into multiple music halls of fame.

88

THE BOY WHO WOULD BE KING

A fresh-faced 21-year-old Elvis Presley is pictured here, on the brink of worldwide fame, during a recording session for RCA in 1956. Before this he had been with Sun Records and enjoyed a few hits in the country charts. Unusually he is playing the piano, rather than his trademark guitar. Whichever instrument he used, he played by ear as he was unable to read music and had no formal musical training whatsoever.

HITTING THE ROAD

This poster is from one of the first shows Elvis did after signing with RCA.

The Jordanaires, billed here as his backing vocalists, went on to work with Elvis for the next 14 years, both in the studio and for live appearances. The quartet, originally formed as a gospel group in 1948, were also featured in some of his films and during many television appearances.

HEARTBREAK HOTEL

While Elvis's early recordings with Sun Records had brought him some success in the South, from Florida to Texas, his first single with RCA, Heartbreak Hotel released on January 27, 1956, became a colossal hit around the world. As well as propelling Elvis to instant stardom, the song made an incredible impact on many of the mega-star musicians who would follow in his wake, including The Beatles. Paul McCartney described the recording as nothing less than the most important artistic creation of the modern era, while John Lennon famously mooted the thought that; "Without Elvis, there would be no Beatles".

MEMORIAL AUDITORIUM
BUFFALO, NY. ★ 8:00 P.M.
SAT., JAN. 21 - 1956

ELVIS
PRESLEY   JORDANAIRES
"Tickets $1.75 - All Seats Reserved"

89

SHAKING THINGS UP

With Heartbreak Hotel having spent seven weeks at number one, Elvis was hot property at the time of this concert in Charlotte, North Carolina. Nationally networked television appearances had helped him build on his recording success – and he proved a natural performer.

The camera loved him. His trademark wiggling, quivering, shaking and pelvis-thrusting style earned him the nickname 'Elvis the Pelvis' and led to outrage and controversy as some journalists and older viewers considered his gyrating hips to be improper, even obscene. This led to his sometimes being filmed for television from the waist up. But in concert no such censoring was possible! Elvis was central to the birth of rock and roll and the kids loved it – although their parents were appalled.

90

IN PERSON!

ELVIS PRESLEY SHOW

CHARLOTTE COLISEUM   CHARLOTTE, N.C.

TUESDAY, JUNE 26, 1956

Show 8:30 p.m.   Doors open 7:00 p.m.

GENERAL ADMISSION TICKET

ADMISSION: IN ADVANCE $1.25

AT DOOR 1.50

Federal State and Local Taxes, if any, included

SHOW RAIN OR SHINE   NO REFUNDS

Nº 3566

ELVIS PRESLEY
Sensational new RCA-Victor
Star - In Person

ELVIS THE BRAND

It is hard to overstate the impact Elvis Presley made on late 1950s America. His talent and voice combined with good looks, sex appeal and electrifying, energetic performances brought him phenomenal fame and attention.

Fan clubs sprang up around the world, with The Official Elvis Presley Fan Club of Great Britain opening in 1957.

A major figure behind his success was his manager, Colonel Tom Parker – a hard taskmaster, deal-maker extraordinaire and a marketing marvel who found new ways to turn Elvis into a brand. It is said that he even thought of making money out of people who weren't fans of his boy by selling 'I Hate Elvis' badges.

1956 LOVE ME TENDER

With Elvis's profile and fame now rocketing, his attentions turned to the big screen and he made his debut as an actor in the black and white western film Love Me Tender released in November 1956. Originally to be called 'The Reno Brothers', (who fall in love with the same girl) the title was changed to capitalise on the success of the pre-released single Love Me Tender, a song from the film which Elvis sang on the popular Ed Sullivan Show during a break from filming. Advance sales of the single passed one million – it went on to sell two million – and was the first case of a single receiving a gold disc before it was released.

After less than a year of mass media exposure, Elvis became a rock and roll icon known all around the world.

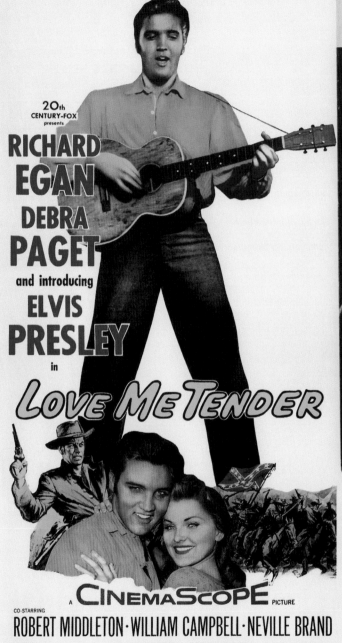

MR. ROCK 'N' ROLL IN THE STORY HE WAS BORN TO PLAY!

20th CENTURY-FOX presents

RICHARD EGAN
DEBRA PAGET
and introducing
ELVIS PRESLEY
in

Love Me Tender

A CINEMASCOPE PICTURE

CO-STARRING
ROBERT MIDDLETON · WILLIAM CAMPBELL · NEVILLE BRAND
WITH MILDRED DUNNOCK · BRUCE BENNETT

PRODUCED BY DAVID WEISBART · DIRECTED BY ROBERT D. WEBB · SCREENPLAY BY ROBERT BUCKNER · BASED ON A STORY BY MAURICE GERAGHTY

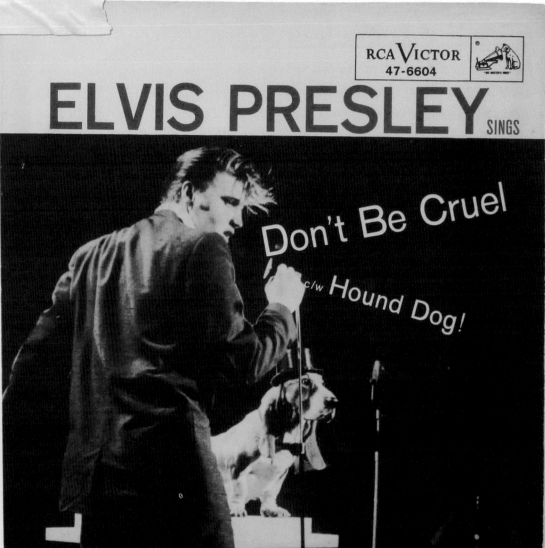

RCA Victor
47-6604

ELVIS PRESLEY sings

Don't Be Cruel
c/w Hound Dog!

© RCA Printed in U. S. A.

91

THE HITS KEEP COMING

His other major hit single in 1956 was the double A-side Don't Be Cruel / Hound Dog which topped the American pop charts for 11 weeks – a record that stood for 36 years – while also simultaneously number one on the US country and R&B charts. By 1958 the single became only the third song in history to sell more than 3 million copies, after Bing Crosby's White Christmas and Gene Autry's Rudolph the Red-Nosed Reindeer. It is Elvis' best-selling song of all.

ON THE ROAD TO SUCCESS

1957 was a pivotal year for Elvis. Now an established superstar, he continued his gruelling schedule of concerts around the United States to huge acclaim and, of course, financial reward. In the spring of 1957, aged just 22, he bought the house and grounds of Graceland in Memphis, Tennessee, for just over $100,000. Elvis and his house became inextricably linked – Graceland was his main home for the next 20 years and remains a major tourist attraction after his death.

92

JAILHOUSE ROCK

Continuing his string of hits, Elvis released the sensational Jailhouse Rock – the title track of his third movie – in September 1957.

Jailhouse Rock, the main number in the film, saw Elvis, clad in stripes and denim, performing at his lip-snarling, knee-quivering best during an elaborate prison dance number which became one of the highlights of his movie career.

The song spent seven weeks at number one in the US and was the first Elvis single to enter the UK charts at number one, where it stayed for three weeks following its UK release in early 1958.

NOW

M-G-M
Presents

ELVIS PRES
IN
JAILHOUSE

Co-starring **JUDY TYLER** ★   Directed by **RICHARD T**

With **MICKEY SHAUGHNESSY**
DEAN JONES   **JENNIFER HOLDEN**

Screen Play by **GUY TROSPER**

in

CINEMASCOPE . . . AN AVON PRODUCTION

HEAR

RCA VICT

KING CREOLE

Elvis won the lead role in King Creole following the death of James Dean, the actor originally cast. Elvis plays a singer on Bourbon Street in New Orleans who gets mixed up with the mob. The big hits from the successful soundtrack were the title track King Creole, Hard Headed Woman and Trouble. Many critics consider this to be Elvis' best acting performance.

Elvis would go on to make a total of 31 films as an actor, but for the time being his performances on stage and screen were brought to an abrupt halt at the height of his fame on March 24 1958 when, despite being one of the most famous entertainers in the country, he joined the US Army.

NOW

LEY ROCK

Produced by PANDRO S. BERMAN

ELVIS PRESLEY
Sing Title Song
"JAILHOUSE ROCK"
AND OTHER SONG HITS!

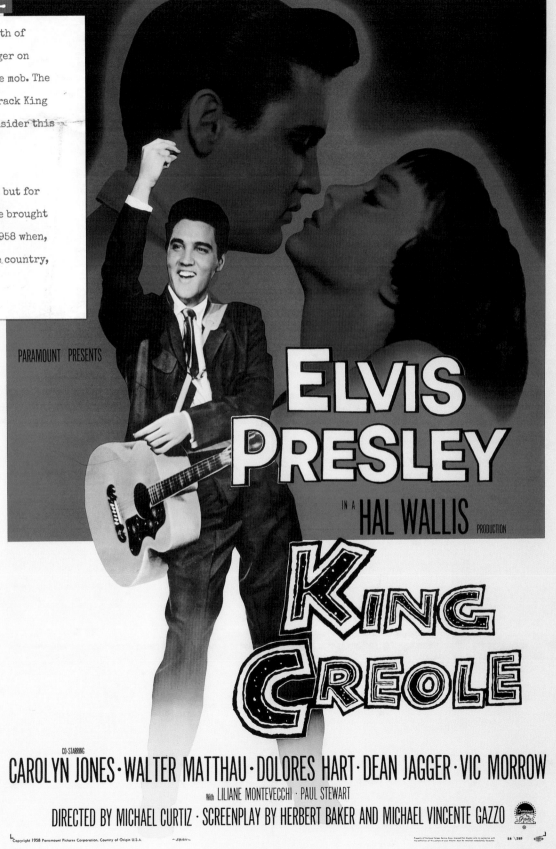

PARAMOUNT PRESENTS

ELVIS PRESLEY

IN A HAL WALLIS PRODUCTION

King Creole

CO-STARRING
CAROLYN JONES · WALTER MATTHAU · DOLORES HART · DEAN JAGGER · VIC MORROW
WITH LILIANE MONTEVECCHI · PAUL STEWART
DIRECTED BY MICHAEL CURTIZ · SCREENPLAY BY HERBERT BAKER AND MICHAEL VINCENTE GAZZO

Copyright 1958 Paramount Pictures Corporation. Country of Origin U.S.A.

93

ACKNOWLEDGEMENT OF SERVICE OBLIGATION

I, _____Elvis Aron Presley_____, HAVING BEEN INDUCTED INTO

THE ARMED SERVICES OF THE UNITED STATES ON THIS _____24th_____ DAY OF

__March_____ 19__58, FOR 2 YEARS ACTIVE DUTY, ACKNOWLEDGE THAT I HAVE

B EEN INFORMED OF MY SERVICE OBLIGATION. I UNDERSTAND THAT UPON COMPLETION

OF MY TERM OF ACTIVE DUTY I WILL, IF QUALIFIED, BE TRANSFERRED TO THE

RESERVE AND REQUIRED TO SERVE THEREIN FOR A PERIOD WHICH, WHEN ADDED TO MY

ACTIVE DUTY SERVICE, TOTALS 6 YEARS, UNLESS SOONER DISCHARGED IN ACCORDANCE

WITH STANDARDS PRESCRIBED B Y THE SECRETARY OF DEFENSE: THAT I WILL BE

REQUIRED TO SERVE A PERIOD IN THE READY RESERVE WHICH, WHEN ADDED TO MY

ACTIVE DUTY SERVICE TOTALS 5 YEARS: THAT I MAY THEN, UPON WRITTEN REQUEST,

BE TRANSFERRED TO THE STANDBY RESERVE FOR THE REMAINDER OF MY OBLIGATED

PERIOD OF SERVICE. I FURTHER UNDERSTAND THAT DURING MY SERVICE AS A MEMBER

OF THE READY RESERVE I WILL BE REQUIRED TO ATTEND NOT LESS THAN 48 SCHEDULE

DRILLS OR TRAINING PERIODS AND NOT MORE THAN 17 DAYS ACTIVE DUTY FOR TRAININ

ANNUALLY, OR THAT IN LIEU THEREOF, WHEN AUTHORIZED, I MAY BE REQUIRED TO

PERFORM 30 DAYS ACTIVE DUTY FOR TRAINING ANNUALLY, THAT FAILURE TO PERFORM

REQUIRED TRAINING IN ANY YEAR CAN RESULT IN MY BEING ORDERED TO PERFORM

ADDITIONAL ACTIVE DUTY FOR TRAINING FOR 45 DAYS FOR THAT YEAR, AND IN

HAVING MY SERVICE IN THE READY RESERVE EXTENDED INVOLUNTARILY.

Elvis A Presley

Pvt E-1 Elvis Aron Presley
US- 53 310 761

IN THE ARMY

When Elvis was drafted into the services he was offered several special roles in recognition of his unusual status as soldier/superstar, including the chance simply to entertain the troops. But Elvis was a patriot and turned down all suggestions involving special treatment because he wanted to serve as a regular soldier in the army. Apart from requesting a deferment to finish filming King Creole, Elvis asked for no other dispensations. He even lost his trademark 'Pompadour-style quiff and had the regular GI haircut. At the time the US was not involved in any conflicts or wars and Elvis was stationed in Germany for two years. He was honourably discharged from active duty on March 5, 1960, receiving a mustering-out check of $109.54. He went straight back to work and filmed, of course, GI Blues.

AT THE MOVIES

There was no letup in filming for Elvis during the 1960s when Colonel Parker decided to take him off the road and make him a movie star. Beginning with Flaming Star in 1960 and ending with Change of Habit in 1969, Elvis made 26 films in the 60s, often as many as three in one year and many critics feel this rapid production cycle adversely affected his music. Over a dozen of the films were basically vehicles for a soundtrack album – many of which appear now in 'worst album' lists. However Blue Hawaii in 1961 is among the happy exceptions. Coming second only to the soundtrack of West Side Story as the most successful album of the 1960s, it includes Can't Help Falling in Love, which was to become an Elvis standard.

MARRIAGE TO PRISCILLA

While stationed in Friedberg, Germany, Elvis met Priscilla Beaulieu who he went on to marry in Las Vegas on May 1, 1967. Elvis was 24 and already a star when he first met 14-year-old Priscilla, so their relationship was unusual from the start.

The couple had their only child, Lisa Marie, in 1968, but went on to divorce in 1972, at Priscilla's instigation. She reportedly found it hard to live in the Elvis 'bubble' surrounded by staff and acolytes. Elvis was said to be devastated and remained close to Priscilla who, together with Lisa Marie, still curates Graceland and is involved in Elvis tributes and his posthumous career.

95

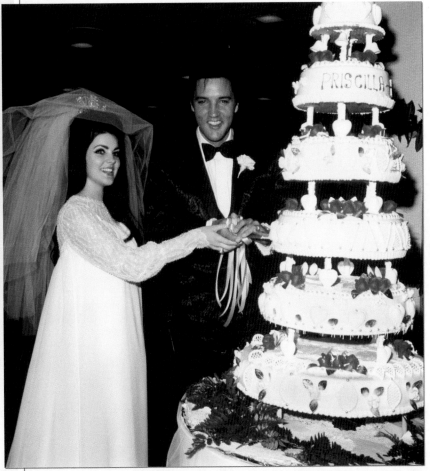

BACK IN BUSINESS

By the late 1960s Elvis was aware his career was in trouble. His increasingly formulaic and cheesy films made him seem quaint and completely out of kilter with popular American music of the time which had become increasingly linked to protest and popular causes including feminism, civil rights and unrest around the Vietnam war. The Beatles, psychedelic rock and Memphis soul had taken over the charts and Elvis hadn't had a number one record since 1962 and not even a top 10 single since 1965.

His 1968 TV special 'Singer presents..... Elvis' — now better known as the '68 Comeback Special' — aired on December 3 and transformed his ailing career. It was his first live performance in seven years and a huge success. The show's soundtrack album made the Top 10 and went platinum, and the single 'If I Can Dream', which he sang at the end of the show, made number 12 in the charts and went gold. Elvis had re-established his credentials — viewers saw him play an electric guitar for the first time — and reminded fans of just what they had been missing. It was the reboot his career needed.

1969 hit releases include In the Ghetto, which reached number three in the US charts and Suspicious Minds which reached number one and was the last chart topper he would have during his lifetime.

THE LAS VEGAS YEARS

Now back in business, Elvis kickstarted the next stage of his career in Las Vegas in July 1969 with the first of what were to become legendary residencies. This debut residency was huge for Elvis and he was incredibly nervous before the first show.

He had no need to worry — the shows were hugely successful and helped him achieve more hit singles and further fame. Accepting that his rock and roll days were over, Elvis reinvented himself as a balladeer and aimed at a more mature audience. He went for a richer, fuller sound during the 1970s, using strong vibrato and adding a gospel flavour to his performances.

His rapport with audiences was strong and he often reminisced about the early days. Altogether he played more than 700 performances in Las Vegas between 1969 and 1976.

BACK ON THE ROAD AGAIN

With his career reinvigorated and back on track, Elvis' work pattern during the 1970s involved a hectic mix of touring the United States and performing in Las Vegas.

Back on the road in February 1970, his first appearances were in Texas where he performed to more than 200,000 fans across six shows at the Houston Astrodome. The 'southern boy' had come to embody Americana and had a new trademark look – the black leather of his youth being replaced by the iconic high-collared, caped and bejewelled jumpsuit.

A musical documentary 'Elvis on Tour' was filmed during the first of three tours he made in 1972. This became a huge success and was the only Elvis film to win an award – the Golden Globe for Best Documentary of 1972.

Although he never again dominated the charts in the way he had in the 1950s, Elvis did have hits in the 1970s. Top 10 singles in the US and the UK included 'The Wonder of You' and 'Burning Love'.

97

DEAR MR PRESIDENT

A bizarre meeting between Elvis and US President Richard Nixon has spawned much debate and even a 'mockumentary' film. The photograph of the event in December 1970 remains one the most-requested shots in the entire US National Archives.

On November 21, Elvis hand-delivered a five-page letter that he'd written on American Airlines stationery to the White House. It began; "Dear Mr. President, First, I would like to introduce myself. I am Elvis Presley and admire you and have great respect for your office."

The letter went on to describe his concern about the problems faced by the United States as he saw it, including 'the drug culture', 'communist brainwashing' and 'the hippie elements' and expressed his desire to help by being appointed a 'Federal Agent at Large.' He concluded by saying he would love to meet 'if you are not too busy'.

Writing later in her memoir 'Elvis and Me' Priscilla Presley said that what he really wanted was a badge from the Federal Bureau of Narcotics and Dangerous Drugs which he believed would then allow him to legally enter any country, carrying any guns and drugs he wished.

Of course Elvis famously never performed outside America, other than during his military service. But a meeting duly took place and Elvis got a badge for his collection. In return he presented the president with a Colt.45 pistol.

American Airlines

In Flight…

Altitude;

Location;

Dear Mr. President.

First I would like to introduce myself.

I am Elvis Presley and admire you

and Have Great Respect for your

office. I talked to Vice President

agnew in Palm Springs 3 weeks and

expressed my concern for our Country.

The Drug Culture, The Hippie Elements,

The SDS, Black Panthers, etc do not

consider me as their enemy or as they

call it the Establishment. I call it america and

ALOHA FROM HAWAII

Aloha from Hawaii was a 1973 concert broadcast worldwide by satellite because, as Colonel Parker claimed at the time; 'It is impossible for us to play in every major city'. What no one knew then, including Elvis himself, was that Parker was actually an illegal immigrant who had arrived in America from Holland after jumping ship and feared he wouldn't get back into the United States if he ever left it. He apparently turned down massive offers for Elvis to appear outside America to protect his secret.

Elvis Presley holds a press conference at the Las Vegas Hilton Hotel to announce his upcoming concert 'Aloha from Hawaii'

99

CURTAIN COMING DOWN

Elvis and Vegas were a match made in heaven, but he also still toured the US. The May 30 concert in Asheville, North Carolina was cancelled and rescheduled for August 26 – but of course then never happened as Elvis died on August 16.

His June 1977 tour was the last he would ever perform and has since become known as the Elvis Final Farewell.

Now aged 42, Elvis had put on weight and was addicted to prescription drugs – depressants to help him sleep when he was hyped up after a show and then stimulants to get him going.

AISLE · SEC 13 · ROW Q · SEAT 12 · JUNE 26, 1977

IN CONCERT
ELVIS
MARKET SQUARE ARENA
INDIANAPOLIS, IND.
SUNDAY
Doors Open – 7:00 PM
SHOWTIME – 8:30 PM
$15.00

ADMIT ONE ON ABOVE DATE ONLY
NO REFUND · NO EXCHANGE

SEC 13 · ROW Q · SEAT 12 · AISLE

THE KING IS DEAD

Elvis was booked seven days a week, sometimes for two shows a day and this tough schedule, combined with the high energy performances he produced, would have punished an artist half his age. By now he was overweight and puffy-looking, often appearing breathless during his shows.

His very last performance was June 26, 1977 at the Market Square Arena, Indianapolis, Indiana.

Less than two months later, on the eve of another tour, Elvis passed away in his Memphis mansion, Graceland, aged 42. The singer was found by his girlfriend, 21-year-old Ginger Alden, unconscious on the floor of the master suite bathroom during the afternoon of August 16, 1977. He was taken to hospital but attempts to revive him failed. The official cause of death was 'cardiac arrhythmia due to undetermined heartbeat', although later reports stated that dangerously high levels of drugs were detected in his body.

The world had lost one of its biggest stars. But his popularity has hardly faded - his music still sells, his mansion gets thousands of visitors a year and Elvis impersonators make a great living. Long live the King.

100

FINAL THE COMMERCIAL

138th Year   No. 229   Memphis, Tenn., Wednesday Morning, August

Death Captures Crown Of
—Elvis Dies Apparently A

By LAWRENCE BUSER

Elvis Presley died Tuesday, apparently after a heart attack, at Graceland Mansion. The 42-year-old 'king of rock and roll' was found unconscious in his night clothes at 2:30 p.m.

Presley was found by his road manager, Joe Esposito, and was taken by ambulance to Baptist Hospital's emergency room where he was pronounced dead at 3:30 p.m., police said. Hospital officials announced the death at 4 p.m.

Esposito told authorities he could find no sign that Presley was breathing and could not detect a heartbeat. He began emergency resuscitation efforts and called a Memphis Fire Department ambulance.

Shelby County Medical Examiner Jerry Francisco, who performed an autopsy, said the death was due to "an erratic heartbeat" but added that the exact cause of death may never be determined.

"There was severe cardiovascular disease present," Dr. Francisco told newsmen Tuesday night after the autopsy was performed. "He had a history of mild hypertension and some coronary artery disease. These two diseases may be responsible for cardiac arrythmia, but the precise cause was not determined. Basically it was a natural death. The precise cause of death may never be discovered."

Initial police reports yesterday said homicide officers were investigating the possibility of death from a heart attack or from an accidental overdose of drugs.

Francisco said, however, there was "no indication of any drug abuse of any kind." He said the only evidence of drugs involved those Presley was taking for his physical condition — mild hypertension and a colon problem.

Francisco said there would have been evidence of needle tracks in his arms or other parts of his body if illegal drugs were involved. He said there would have been evidence in or on his nose if cocaine had been involved.

He said death occurred between 9 a.m. and 2 p.m. "There's no precise than that," Fran

Dr. George Nichopoul sonal physician, said las aware of "anything he d day (Monday)" and sai Ginger Alden" was the 2:15 p.m. or 2:30 p.m.

As news of Presley's grams and phone calls b Memphis from mourner throughout the world wis press condolences to Pr or to arrange lodging to or both. Radio stations b music and record stores

Elvis Went From Rags To Riches

By WILLIAM THOMAS

He was born in a two-room house in Tupelo, Miss., on Jan. 8, 1935, a nobody with a somebody destiny.

He was the twin who lived — the son of Vernon and Gladys Presley, who had been married two years earlier in Verona, Miss., amidst the Great Depression.

"We matched their names," his mother recalled later, "Jesse Garon and Elvis Aron. Jesse died at birth. Maybe that is why Elvis is so dear to us."

For the next 13 years, the Presleys struggled for survival in Mississippi. Vernon Presley farmed while his wife toiled in shirt and dress factories. They moved to Memphis in 1948, but things didn't get better — at least not right away.

Mrs. Presley worked as a nurses' aide at St. Joseph Hospital. Elvis enrolled in L.O. Humes High School and worked as an usher in a movie theater.

Briefly, he went out for the football team but had to quit in order to go to work.

Although the family was so poor that they had to accept a charity Christmas basket during the holidays, Presley managed to graduate from high school in 1953 and land a job as a truck driver at $35 a week.

By then, however, he had developed a

He

'Are Yo
—The

By TERRY K
and OTIS L. SA

A sad, quiet crowd of a gathered at the emergenc of Baptist Hospital minut

A massive heart attack at mansion

'King of Rock' Dead at 42

APPEAL FINAL

ck And Roll
r Heart Attack

other parts of the country reported a run on Elvis records.

Memphis Mayor Wyeth Chandler said flags on all city buildings would be flown at half staff until the funeral.

Police said they were told Presley had played racketball at his home early Tuesday and quit about 6 a.m. when he told friends he was going to read.

Esposito found Presley in his night clothes in his second-floor bathroom. He said he could find no sign of breathing or heartbeat and immediately summoned an ambulance.

Nichopoulos was performing cardio-pulmonary resuscitation when the ambulance

arrived shortly after 2:30 p.m.

A Memphis Fire Department ambulance from Engine House 29 at 2147 Elvis Presley Boulevard responded to the call at 2:33 p.m. and by 2:56 p.m. had taken Presley to the emergency room at Baptist Hospital in Midtown from his Whitehaven home seven miles away.

Martin Davis of Chattanooga, a construction projects engineer with K-Mart Discount Stores, said he was driving south on Elvis Presley Boulevard when an ambulance almost hit him as it turned into the driveway at Graceland.

"The ambulance damn near ran over me," he said. "It hit the gate as it was
(Continued on Page 12)

Elvis is dead at 42

MEMPHIS, Tenn. (AP) — Elvis Presley, the Mississippi boy whose rock and roll guitar and gyrating hips launched a new style in popular music, died Tuesday afternoon at Baptist Hospital, police said. He was 42.

Presley, who parlayed a $4 trip to a recording studio into a multi-million dollar business, was taken to the emergency room of Baptist Hospital, suffering from what hospital officials said was respiratory distress.

Dr. George C. Nichopoulos, Presley's personal physician, said that a heart attack was a possible cause of death, but that he could not be sure until after a post mortem.

Capt. John McLaughlin of the Memphis Police Department denied an earlier report that detectives were investigating a possible drug overdose.

"We are not investigating the use of drugs." said McLaughlin. "I don't know where that information came from but it's not so."

Hundreds of people gathered at the hospital and at Presley's Gra-

Hospital officials said the entertainer was found unconscious at his home by his road manager, Joe Esposito.

Esposito began resuscitation efforts and called a fire department ambulance. Emergency medical technicians with the ambulance continued cardiopulmonary resuscitation efforts on the way to the hospital.

Nichopoulos halted resuscitation attempts at about 3:30 p.m. (4:30 p.m. EDT), according to the hospital.

Presley had been a frequent patient at the hospital over the past few years.

When he was rumored to be suffering from various incurable diseases, his physicians had blamed his hospitalizations on eye trouble, a twisted colon and on exhaustion.

Earlier this year, he cancelled several performances in Louisiana and returned to Memphis where he was hospitalized for what his physicians said was exhaustion.

He had rarely been seen in public recently, and his weight was said to have ballooned

an 11-day tour to begin Wednesday in Portland, Maine.

Presley's gyrating hips were only mildly suggestive compared to most of today's rock performers. But when he appeared on the Ed Sullivan Show in the 1950's, fears his sexuality seemed so overt that he was shown only from the waist up.

"Everytime I move on television, they write that I'm obscene," Presley once said. "I've seen a lot worse movements than mine every night on TV. Look at all that modern dancing. If I did those movements, they'd want to lynch me. Yet I never read anything criticizing modern ballet."

His shake, rattle and roll showmanship — with such million sellers as "You Ain't Nothing But A Hound Dog," "Heartbreak Hotel," "Blue Suede Shoes" and "Love Me Tender," kept teen-age girls sighing.

He performed with slicked back hair, sideburns and a perpetual sneer.

Presley went from driving a

101

Body Of Elvis Presley Fron

re There's I
ired Answe

announcement that earlier reports been wrong.

"Are you sure?" asked Winston 63, of 1875 Mignon. "Have you confir it for sure? There's no mistake?"

Memphis Leads World in Mourning
For Elvis Presley

By CHARLES GOODMAN
and HENRY BAILEY
Press-Scimitar Staff Writers

A slow mist fell on the quiet crowd at the gate in front of Graceland today. They waited — it was all they could do now — for the hearse that would bring their king, Elvis Presley, for his final hours at home.

Then came flashing yellow lights and a rising moan of sirens, and a caravan swept in a side entrance of the grounds to avoid the crowd, which had surged forward. A hearse entered behind police motorcycles, and the crowd watched as a copper casket was carried up the steps of Graceland and in the front door.

It was six minutes past noon.

"Elvis is really dead," someone said huskily. "Why did he have to leave us?"

Little else was said in the crowd, which on the day after Elvis' death had grown steadily in size in anticipation of a public visitation from 3 to 5 p.m. in Graceland. The casket was to be open for those paying final tribute.

Private funeral services will be at 2 p.m. tomorrow at Graceland, with entombment in the Forest Hill Cemetery Midtown mausoleum instead of the Presley family plot in the cemetery, a spokesman said.

Well-known personalities were arriving in the city today, including show business celebrities and others, such as Caroline Kennedy, daughter of the late President. Mostly, however, those arriving had unfamiliar names.

Remembering how it all began: Front Row columnist Edwin Howard reprints the first interview with Elvis Presley. Page 36.

He Touched Us All: Reminiscences of Good Evening columnist Bill Burk, Page 7.

Elvis Presley: An editorial, Page 6.

The world mourns; the scene at Graceland yesterday; local commentary on Page 27.

A one-time bodyguard discusses Presley's drug problems. Page 8.

The Presley story in pictures, Page 9.

"I came too late," softly cried Mrs. Gail Peak, who was passing through Memphis to see Graceland, on the way home from vacation with her family. "I loved his music for 25 years, came here to see his home — and now he's dead."

Trembling fingers touched her lips as she looked through the gate and up the winding drive to the mansion.

"The ordinary people want to keep it as a memorial to Elvis. If money were needed, people everywhere would help."

The crowd made way for someone bringing a large spray of roses. Moments later a tall, bearded leather suited member of the Nomad Family rode up on his chopper, dismounted and without a word or a glance, strode up to the gate and tied a black ribbon on the gate. Then he strode back to his chopper and drove away.

Janice Lancaster worked her way through the jammed traffic, moving slow-

ly past Graceland, carrying a coffee pot and cups. She passed out coffee to the crowd.

"It's all I can do for Elvis now," she said. "I want to do something."

One of the crowd, Phillip Foley, 22, of 3577 Tall Oaks, told a national television interviewer, "Elvis stood good in America, something that has moulded our lives. He'll be in our memory until we die. Whether you be black or white, redneck or freak, from Memphis or Moscow, Elvis remains the king. The vibes are too heavy — he's still alive, somehow.

"People aren't here so they can say they were at Graceland the night Elvis died. They're here because it's the only way the common people can pay their respects. We all can't drive up there to the mansion in our limousines but — but we can be here."

Many in the crowds when the clouded light broke over Graceland early this
Turn to Page 10—MOURNERS

ELVIS PRESLEY: THE BEAT WENT ON — AND ON AND ON — UPI Telephoto

DISCOGRAPHY

STUDIO ALBUMS

TITLE	RELEASED	CHART POSITION	
ELVIS PRESLEY	March 23rd 1956	1 (UK)	1 (US)
ELVIS	October 19th 1956	3 (UK)	1 (US)
ELVIS CHRISTMAS ALBUM	October 15th 1957	2 (UK)	1 (US)
FOR LP FANS ONLY	February 6th 1959		19 (US)
A DATE WITH ELVIS	July 24th 1959	4 (UK)	32 (US)
ELVIS IS BACK	April 8th 1960	1 (UK)	2 (US)
HIS HAND IN MINE	November 10th 1960	3 (UK)	13 (US)
SOMETHING FOR EVERYBODY	June 17th 1961	2 (UK)	1 (US)
POT LUCK	June 5th 1962	1 (UK)	4 (US)
HOW GREAT THOU ART	February 27th 1967	11 (UK)	18 (US)
FROM ELVIS IN MEMPHIS	June 17th 1969	1 (UK)	13 (US)
FROM MEMPHIS TO VEGAS / FROM VEGAS TO MEMPHIS	October 14th 1969	3 (UK)	12 (US)
ELVIS COUNTRY (I'M 10,000 YEARS OLD)	January 2nd 1971	6 (UK)	12 (US)
LOVE LETTERS FROM ELVIS	June 16th 1971	7 (UK)	33 (US)
ELVIS SINGS THE WONDERFUL WORLD OF CHRISTMAS	October 20th 1971		
ELVIS NOW	February 20th 1972	12 (UK)	43 (US)
HE TOUCHED ME	April 1972	38 (UK)	79 (US)
ELVIS (THE "FOOL" ALBUM)	July 1973	16 (UK)	52 (US)
RAISED ON ROCK / FOR OL' TIMES SAKE	October 1st 1973		50 (US)
GOOD TIMES	March 20th 1974	42 (UK)	90 (US)
PROMISED LAND	January 8th 1975	21 (UK)	47 (US)
TODAY	May 7th 1975	48 (UK)	57 (US)
FROM ELVIS PRESLEY BOULEVARD MEMPHIS TENNESSEE	May 1st 1976	29 (UK)	41 (US)
MOODY BLUE	July 19th 1977	3 (UK)	3 (US)

LIVE ALBUMS

TITLE	RELEASED	CHART POSITION	
FROM MEMPHIS TO VEGAS / FROM VEGAS TO MEMPHIS	October 14th 1969	3 (UK)	12 (US)
ON STAGE	June 1970	2 (UK)	13 (US)
ELVIS: AS RECORDED AT MADISON SQUARE GARDEN	June 18th 1972	3 (UK)	11 (US)
ALOHA FROM HAWAII VIA SATELLITE	February 4th 1973	11 (UK)	1 (US)
ELVIS RECORDED LIVE ON STAGE IN MEMPHIS	July 7th 1974	44 (UK)	33 (US)
ELVIS IN CONCERT	October 3rd 1977	13 (UK)	5 (US)

SOUNDTRACK ALBUMS

TITLE	RELEASED	CHART POSITION	
LOVING YOU	July 1st 1957	1 (UK)	1 (US)
KING CREOLE	September 19th 1958	1 (UK)	2 (US)
G.I. BLUES	October 1st 1960	1 (UK)	1 (US)
BLUE HAWAII	November 9th 1962	1 (UK)	1 (US)
GIRLS! GIRLS! GIRLS!	November 9th 1962	2 (UK)	3 (US)
IT HAPPENED AT THE WORLD'S FAIR	April 10th 1963	4 (UK)	4 (US)
FUN IN ACAPULCO	November 1st 1963	9 (UK)	3 (US)
KISSIN' COUSINS	April 2nd 1964	5 (UK)	6 (US)
ROUSTABOUT	October 20th 1964	12 (UK)	1 (US)
GIRL HAPPY	March 2nd 1965	8 (UK)	8 (US)
HARUM SCARUM	November 3rd 1965	11 (UK)	8 (US)
FRANKIE AND JOHNNY	March 1st 1966	11 (UK)	20 (US)
PARADISE, HAWAIIAN STYLE	June 10th 1966	7 (UK)	15 (US)
SPINOUT	October 31st 1966	17 (UK)	18 (US)
DOUBLE TROUBLE	June 1st 1967	34 (UK)	47 (US)
CLAMBAKE	October 10th 1967	39 (UK)	40 (US)
SPEEDWAY	May 1st 1968		82 (US)
ELVIS (NBC-TV SPECIAL)	November 22nd 1968	2 (UK)	8 (US)
THAT'S THE WAY IT IS	November 11th 1970	12 (UK)	21 (US)
VIVA ELVIS	November 11th 2010	19 (UK)	48 (US)

103

Singles - US Billboard Hot 100

TITLE	CHART POSITION
1954	
THAT'S ALL RIGHT	
GOOD ROCKIN' TONIGHT	
I DON'T CARE IF THE SUN DON'T SHINE	74 (US Hot)
1955	
BABY LET'S PLAY HOUSE	
MYSTERY TRAIN	
I FORGOT TO REMEMBER TO FORGET	
1956	
HEARTBREAK HOTEL	1 (US Hot)
I WAS THE ONE	19 (US Hot)
BLUE SUEDE SHOES	20 (US Hot)
I WANT TO, I NEED YOU, I LOVE YOU	1 (US Hot)
MY BABY LEFT ME	31 (US Hot)
DON'T BE CRUEL	1 (US Hot)
HOUND DOG	1 (US Hot)
TUTTI-FRUTTI	
I GOT A WOMAN	
I'LL NEVER LET YOU GO (LIL' DARLIN')	
I LOVE YOU BECAUSE	
BLUE MOON	55 (US Hot)
MONEY HONEY	76 (US Hot)
SHAKE RATTLE AND ROLL	
LOVE ME TENDER	1 (US Hot)
ANY WAY YOU WANT ME (THAT'S HOW I WILL BE)	27 (US Hot)
LOVE ME	2 (US Hot)
WHEN MY BLUE MOON TURNS TO GOLD AGAIN	19 (US Hot)
PARALYSED	59 (US Hot)
OLD SHEP	47 (US Hot)
POOR BOY	24 (US Hot)
1957	
TOO MUCH	1 (US Hot)
PLAYING FOR KEEPS	21 (US Hot)
ALL SHOOK UP	1 (US Hot)

104

TITLE	CHART POSITION
THAT'S WHEN YOUR HEARTACHES BEGIN	58 (US Hot)
PEACE IN THE VALLEY	25 (US Hot)
(LET ME BE YOUR) TEDDY BEAR	1 (US Hot)
LOVING YOU	20 (US Hot)
MEAN WOMAN BLUES	
JAILHOUSE ROCK	1 (US Hot)
TREAT ME NICE	18 (US Hot)

1958

DON'T	1 (US Hot)
I BEG OF YOU	8 (US Hot)
WEAR MY RING AROUND YOUR NECK	2 (US Hot)
DONCHA' THINK IT'S TIME	15 (US Hot)
HARDHEADED WOMAN	1 (US Hot)
DON'T ASK ME WHY	25 (US Hot)
ONE NIGHT	4 (US Hot)
I GOT STUNG	8 (US Hot)

1959

(NOW AND THEN THERE'S) A FOOL SUCH AS I	2 (US Hot)
I NEED YOUR LOVE TONIGHT	4 (US Hot)
A BIG HUNK O' LOVE	1 (US Hot)
MY WISH CAME TRUE	12 (US Hot)

1960

STUCK ON YOU	1 (US Hot)
FAME AND FORTUNE	17 (US Hot)
IT'S NOW OR NEVER	1 (US Hot)
A MESS OF BLUES	32 (US Hot)
ARE YOU LONESOME TONIGHT	1 (US Hot)
I GOTTA KNOW	20 (US Hot)

1961

SURRENDER	1 (US Hot)
LONELY MAN	32 (US Hot)
FLAMING STAR	14 (US Hot)
I FEEL SO BAD	5 (US Hot)
WILD IN THE COUNTRY	26 (US Hot)
(MARIE'S THE NAME) HIS LATEST FLAME	4 (US Hot)
LITTLE SISTER	5 (US Hot)

TITLE	CHART POSITION
CAN'T HELP FALLING IN LOVE	2 (US Hot)

1962

ROCK-A-HULA BABY	23 (US Hot)
GOOD LUCK CHARM	1 (US Hot)
ANYTHING THAT'S PART OF YOU	31 (US Hot)
FOLLOW THAT DREAM	15 (US Hot)
SHE'S NOT YOU	5 (US Hot)
JUST TELL HER JIM SAID HELLO	55 (US Hot)
KING OF THE WHOLE WIDE WORLD	30 (US Hot)
RETURN TO SENDER	2 (US Hot)
WHERE DO YOU COME FROM	99 (US Hot)

1963

ONE BROKEN HEART FOR SALE	11 (US Hot)
THEY REMIND ME TOO MUCH OF YOU	53 (US Hot)
(YOU'RE THE DEVIL IN DISGUISE)	3 (US Hot)
BOSSA NOVA BABY	8 (US Hot)
WITCHCRAFT	32 (US Hot)

106

1964

KISSIN' COUSINS	12 (US Hot)
IT HURTS ME	29 (US Hot)
KISS ME QUICK	34 (US Hot)
SUSPICION	103 (US Hot)
WHAT'D I SAY	21 (US Hot)
VIVA LAS VEGAS	29 (US Hot)
SUCH A NIGHT	16 (US Hot)
NEVER-ENDING	111 (US Hot)
ASK ME	12 (US Hot)
AIN'T THAT LOVING YOU BABY	16 (US Hot)
WOODEN HEART	107 (US Hot)

1965

DO THE CLAM	21 (US Hot)
YOU'LL BE GONE	121 (US Hot)
CRYING IN THE CHAPEL	3 (US Hot)
(SUCH AN) EASY QUESTION	11 (US Hot)
IT FEELS SO RIGHT	55 (US Hot)
I'M YOURS	11 (US Hot)

DISCOGRAPHY

TITLE	CHART POSITION
PUPPET ON A STRING	14 (US Hot)
SANTA CLAUS IS BACK IN TOWN	

1966

TELL ME WHY	33 (US Hot)
BLUE RIVER	95 (US Hot)
JOSHUA FIT THE BATTLE	
MILKY WHITE WAY	
FRANKIE AND JOHNNY	25 (US Hot)
PLEASE DON'T STOP LOVING ME	45 (US Hot)
LOVE LETTERS	19 (US Hot)
COME WHAT MAY	109 (US Hot)
'SPINOUT	40 (US Hot)
ALL THAT I AM	41 (US Hot)
IF EVERY DAY WAS LIKE CHRISTMAS	

1967

INDESCRIBABLY BLUE	33 (US Hot)
FOOLS FALL IN LOVE	102 (US Hot)
LONG LEGGED GIRL (WITH THE SHORT DRESS ON)	63 (US Hot)
THAT'S SOMEONE YOU NEVER FORGET	92 (US Hot)
THERE'S ALWAYS ME	56 (US Hot)
JUDY	78 (US Hot)
BIG BOSS MAN	38 (US Hot)
YOU DON'T KNOW ME	44 (US Hot)

1968

GUITAR MAN	43 (US Hot)
HI-HEEL SNEAKERS	
U.S.MALE	28 (US Hot)
STAY AWAY	67 (US Hot)
YOU'LL NEVER WALK ALONE	90 (US Hot)
WE CALL ON HIM	106 (US Hot)
YOUR TIME HASN'T COME YET BABY	72 (US Hot)
LET YOURSELF GO	71 (US Hot)
A LITTLE LESS CONVERSATION	69 (US Hot)
ALMOST IN LOVE	95 (US Hot)
IF I CAN DREAM	12 (US Hot)
EDGE OF REALITY	112 (US Hot)

TITLE	CHART POSITION
1969	
MEMORIES	35 (US Hot)
HOW GREAT THOU ART	101 (US Hot)
IN THE GHETTO	3 (US Hot)
CLEAN UP YOUR OWN BACKYARD	35 (US Hot)
SUSPICIOUS MINDS	1 (US Hot)
DON'T CRY DADDY	6 (US Hot)
RUBBERNECKIN'	
1970	
KENTUCKY RAIN	16 (US Hot)
THE WONDER OF YOU	9 (US Hot)
MAMA LIKED THE ROSES	
I'VE LOST YOU	32 (US Hot)
THE NEXT STEP IS LOVE	
YOU DON'T HAVE TO SAY YOU LOVE ME	11 (US Hot)
PATCH IT UP	
I REALLY DON'T WANT TO KNOW	21 (US Hot)
THERE GOES MY EVERYTHING	
1971	
RAGS TO RICHES	
WHERE DID THEY GO, LORD	33 (US Hot)
LIFE	53 (US Hot)
ONLY BELIEVE	
I'M LEAVIN'	36 (US Hot)
HEART OF ROME	
IT'S ONLY LOVE	51 (US Hot)
THE SOUND OF YOUR CRY	
MERRY CHRISTMAS BABY	
1972	
UNTIL IT'S TIME FOR YOU TO GO	40 (US Hot)
WE CAN MAKE THE MORNING	
HE TOUCHED ME	
AN AMERICAN TRILOGY	
BURNING LOVE	2 (US Hot)
IT'S A MATTER OF TIME	
SEPARATE WAYS	20 (US Hot)
ALWAYS ON MY MIND	

DISCOGRAPHY

TITLE	CHART POSITION
1973	
STEAMROLLER BLUES	17 (US Hot)
FOOL	
RAISED ON ROCK	41 (US Hot)
FOR OL' TIMES SAKE	
1974	
I'VE GOT A THING ABOUT YOU BABY	39 (US Hot)
TAKE GOOD CARE OF HER	
IF YOU TALK IN YOUR SLEEP	17 (US Hot)
HELP ME	
PROMISED LAND	14 (US Hot)
IT'S MIDNIGHT	
1975	
T-R-O-U-B-L-E	35 (US Hot)
BRINGING IT BACK	65 (US Hot)
PIECES OF MY LIFE	
1976	
HURT	28 (US Hot)
FOR THE HEART	
MOODY BLUE	31 (US Hot)
SHE THINKS I STILL CARE	
1977	
WAY DOWN	18 (US Hot)
PLEDGING MY LOVE	
MY WAY	22 (US Hot)
AMERICA	
1978	
UNCHAINED MELODY	
SOFTLY AS I LEAVE YOU	109 (US Hot)